INTERNET OF THINGS BUSINESS PRIMER

- How to Build an IoT Business

Stanford Edition

BY SUDHA JAMTHE

The Internet of Things Business Primer

Published by Sudha Jamthe

Editor: Hiru Létap

Foreword: Brian Solis

Epilogue: Rob Van Kranenburg

Cover Design: Neha Jamthe

ISBN: 978-1518800627

Book Website: **http://www.iotbusinessprimer.com**

First Published: Dec 2015

DEDICATION

To You Mom

CONTENTS

Foreword by Brian Solis

The Best Things in Life Aren't Things...They're Experiences

You're about to meet my dear friend Sudha. Together over the years, we've helped Silicon Valley businesses, from the Fortune 500 to fledging startups to everything in between, bridge technology solutions to real world users, sparking trends and growing them into significant markets that spanned along the bell curve. The one thing we learned over and over again, is this...technology is not everything as easy as it is to believe otherwise. In the best cases, those where innovation changes user behavior or completely disrupts behavior while making older ways or things obsolete, technology is often an enabler to something bigger than just the product by itself.

Believe it or not, the Valley and its entire ecosystem of investors, entrepreneurs and partners, still need help when it comes to shiny object syndrome...placing inordinate value in popular or trendy tech over longer term vision and possibilities. I call this mediumism. And, while this might sound commonsensical, it is something that's often missed by entrepreneurs and executives alike. Technology should not be the catalyst; it should be the answer. Yet, we get so caught up in hardware, code, competition, potential, challenges, etc., that we may forget to see the user, the person, in our sights and as our source of inspiration and innovation. Truth is, there are too many people with too many ideas and far too much money to fund at least a few rounds of development. *In many ways though, you are not your ultimate customer.*

When it comes to the Internet of Things or the Internet of Everything, this couldn't be truer. Yes, we have incredible products already enhancing our lifestyles, improving how we work, improving our health, upgrading how we discover, altering how we shop and more so transforming industries including but not limited to medical, construction, operations, banking and finance, retail, home automation, intelligence, industrial and the environment.

The thing is that the Internet of Things is just that...things (albeit connected things). But for your work to matter, to really innovate or disrupt, you have to start with a more cohesive and larger vision that appreciates one simple core philosophy, the best things in life aren't things, they're experiences. What you build must enhance something both by itself and part of a larger ecosystem. What you create must be designed to go beyond "things." Instead, design for humans. Design for experiences.

While on stage in 1997 at the Apple WWDC, Steve Jobs was confronted by a developer in the audience who took issue with his approach to bringing change at Apple. In hindsight, Jobs was retaking Apple to shift it from a technology company into a brand that used technology to deliver experiences and more so, connect each experience into a more meaningful and productive experiential universe. As you enjoy this book and your work with Sudha, I'll leave you with the words of Jobs in that moment to remind you of the importance of your work...

"You have to start with the customer experience and work back to technology. You can't start with technology and try to figure out where you're going to sell it. And I've made this mistake more than anybody...and I have the scar tissue to prove it. I know it's is the case. What incredible benefits can we give to the customer? Where can we take the customer? Not starting....with what awesome technology we have and how we're going to market it."

Experience is everything.

- Brian Solis, digital analyst, anthropologist, futurist – author of X, The Experience When Business Meets Design

SUDHA JAMTHE

CHAPTER 1: Introduction

1.1 Audience

This book is for –

My Stanford students to get a strong foundation about Internet of Things (IoT) and to learn to break down an IoT Product as a Business Application.

Entrepreneurs who want to build Mobile and IoT businesses.

Technology Strategists, Product Managers, Business Analysts and Business Process Managers looking for in-depth analysis of the impact of Internet of Things on their industries.

Hardware, software and networking professionals who want to understand the spectrum of IoT applications and learn what it takes to go from an IoT device idea to an IoT Business.

Students to understand where are the jobs in IoT and what skills are needed to get those jobs.

Anyone wondering if IoT is a hype or real yearning to learn what is out there and draw inspiration from the early adopters.

1.2 How is This Book Organized?

This book is organized into five parts.

Part I covers the strategic approach to **building an IoT Business from a technology idea**. This section is particularly important for Product Strategists and Product Managers. It covers **how to extend an existing business using IoT or create a new business**. You will also learn to **optimize the Customer Experience across multi-device** customer touch points.

Part II offers an in-depth look at **Internet of Things applications** ranging from consumer applications such as **wearables, smart cities and connected cars to industrial and manufacturing applications**. This is a methodical discussion of challenges and best practices in building and launching IoT applications with case studies of current IoT Businesses. In this section, you will also learn what is '**Machine to Machine' (M2M)**.

Part III covers **disruptive innovations from Internet of Things across industries and the evolving best practices of value creation**. In this section you will get an in-depth analysis about top three industries **healthcare, retail and education.** We will look at proximity sensors (**Beacons)** and the difference between Beacon deployment standards for iOS and Android and a case study on the application of beacons by several global **retailers in stores, malls and airports**. Finally you will be introduced to innovative disruptions impacting product brochures and **education** industries making the transition from paper to electronics using IoT to bridge the gap.

Part IV will cover technologies that make up the IoT ecosystem that have a strategic impact on the business you build. I cover **Big Data, Predictive Analytics, Data Science** and how value is created from IoT data. This is a fast growing area of IoT adoption and you will learn methods as well as data applications that you could apply to your business.

Part V is about the future of IoT. First we start with a section on **IoT jobs**. Then, I will share mind-blowing examples that are pushing the human machine boundary with the merger of **IoT and Artificial Intelligence and affective computing**. I will cover **Bio Payments and Augmented reality**. I hope you derive inspiration as much as knowledge from this section.

1.3 What are Internet of Things Devices and Products?

My car broke down and I rushed to take it for service before the dealer closed for the weekend. I left home and forgot to close my garage and rushed back to double check and close it. While I waited for my car I remembered we had run out of pet food, soap and coffee and did a run to the market to buy them. I came home and found that I had locked myself out and had left my keys inside. I called my spouse for my spare keys. We have to keep track of so many things because all things all around us are un-smart.

I wish I lived in a world where my car would take care of its own service; my garage would close automatically when I leave home, and my household appliances would order refills.

This is not a futuristic world.

It gets even better. My home would know when I enter and unlock doors for me and lights would turn on automatically. It will even know if I returned after a workout and turn my thermostat to a comfortable setting. My pet feeder would have fed my cat and she will nuzzle around my feet. In the morning my alarm will tell the coffeemaker and toaster when I am getting up so my breakfast will be ready for me.

Internet of Things (IoT) has begun creating this convenient world for us by making ordinary things we carry on us and around us smart by adding sensors to track and fix problems before they arise. This opens us to a whole new world of conveniences not earlier possible when our toothbrush and toasters just did their boring old mechanical actions.

I would call IoT transformative because it is changing our world to run so smoothly and disrupting many industries. The transformation from an IoT business comes from the beauty that you could make an IoT device with a sensor into many different products. I could make a device that measures hydration levels and build it out to a product that keeps our plants hydrated and you could build the same device into a product that keeps a baby's butt dry.

Join me to learn how to take an IoT device and turn it into an IoT Product and transform it into an IoT Business. Let's take an in-depth look at how to create new businesses and markets for existing businesses to build the new convenient world.

1.4 IoT Technologies Overview

Imagine your garage opener. Prior to IoT, we pushed a remote button and voilà it opened your garage. This was proprietary communication between the mechanical remote and the garage door using RF communication with a Radio transmitter, similar to how our telephone handset communicates to its base.

By making the garage a smart IoT device, the same push of the garage button happens from a mobile App that communicates to the garage via the Internet using Wi-Fi or Bluetooth and magically transforms a software electric signal to a mechanical switch to open or close the garage. In laymen language the IoT smart garage monitors itself whether it was left open beyond a certain pre-set threshold time and notifies the user who can remotely close it and continue on her jolly way. In technology terms it is a miracle to get an electric pulse from a software app to create a mechanical movement in a faraway garage hub to make it close the garage. I am not even getting into how the garage monitored itself for being left open and sent a notification to a software app far away.

Join me in marveling at the layers of technologies. It includes embedded devices, communication with Bluetooth or Wi-Fi, security software, data analytics, cloud infrastructure, notifications, integration of hardware and software, cool consumer designs, intelligent programmatic actions, mobile software app, chip and system processing power converting between electric microprocessor signals to mechanical switch or relay movement to make our device do what it did manually.

1.5 Market Size and Value Creation

'There will between 26 to 50 Billion IoT devices in the world by 2020 [1] which translates to 6 devices per person on the planet.

By 2018 companies that started 3 years earlier will provide 50% of IoT solutions. [2]

This means that companies starting now are going to offer 50% of all IoT solutions in 2 years from now, on their way to serving a world of 50 Billion IoT devices in 2020. IoT growth is led by product innovations and cost efficiencies.

Value is created with IoT devices at the sensors, at the communication layer by sharing information to users to take near real-time action and by analytics insights. For example in the sensors in the Amazon Dash IoT Device signal the depletion of pet supply and re-ordering them creates value. In Boeing, where sensors signal faulty equipment and communicate it real-time to get the aircraft fixed quickly, the value is created in the communication. In Healthcare, the analysis of a patient's health data integrated with their health history saves lives creating value in the analytics insights. So it is important for a product manager to know where value is created in a Product and develop the best customer experience that optimizes this full value for the customer.

1.6 Building an IoT Business

The term IoT refers to enterprise and consumer products. Entrepreneurs come up with an idea to solve a particular problem such as helping a user run with better posture or for kids to brush their teeth well. They typically build an IoT device which is a piece of hardware with power, add some sensors to it, add Internet access and collect data to drive some action.

It is important to note that an IoT device does not make an IoT product. As the first step, you should figure out who is the customer for your product.

Customers experience a product through multiple touch points. The product design is the first communication with your customer. For IoT products customers experience the product from the industrial design of the hardware, software user flows and their experience setting up the Internet connectivity. So it is important to create a seamless customer experience across all touch points that communicates the problem solved and value offered by your IoT Product.

Then it is important to market validate the customer's need solved by your product and adapt your product design to the customer's feedback. Then build this into a full business with a business model, distribution channels, and plans to build out the production version of the product for deployment.

We will cover how to build an IoT Product as a new business or extend an existing business into new markets using IoT in Part I.

1.7 What does IoT offer you the Product Manager?

Overall IoT has been gaining adoption with open source developers, large companies and many startups reintroducing devices all around us, on our bodies, homes, cars and cities creating the next wave of value from the Internet to create new conveniences.

IoT creates

- New opportunity for Entrepreneurs, Product Managers and Technology Business Managers to innovate in many different industries to create cost efficiencies and to create whole new value from conveniences not perceived possible before.

- New challenges for Product Designers in imagining an integrated customer experience across hardware and software touch points.

- A world of possibilities to create value from vast data from sensors and the challenge in presenting insights with simplicity to create optimal customer engagement.

- Opportunities for new open data sets across cities of the world to create community engagement to improve lives of citizens.

- A threat for many existing businesses that do not look beyond their current market boundaries

- Opportunities for entrepreneurs and product managers to expand existing businesses to new markets.

- Questions about customer data privacy and security for each Product Manager to answer in their Product Design.

PART I:
BUILDING AN
IoT BUSINESS

"Building an IoT Business is different from any other business because it requires a wide range of competency in one startup - industrial design, software development on cloud and mobile, manufacturing at scale, marketing, sales, logistics and building amazing teams" - **Thomas Serval, CEO Kolibree**

CHAPTER 2: IoT Product as a Business Application

2.1 A Device is not a Product

An IoT device is made of hardware and sensors. An IoT Product on the other hand is a device with a customer experience focused on solving a problem for the customer.

In fact the same device can be built out into many different products.

For example you could make a device that measures temperature changes using a thermal sensor. If it measures the temperature of a baby it becomes a baby thermometer. If it measures the inside of a room, it becomes a home thermostat like Nest. If it measures the temperature of a boiler it becomes a boiler safety product in a factory. If instead of a baby it measures the temperature of an adult as they wear it on them it becomes an adult wearable product. If it measures the temperature of a liquid, it becomes a product such as a Water Glass, which helps you stay hydrated tracking how much water you drank.

So, what does it take to make a product from a device?

2.2 Three steps to make an IoT Product

1. Know your Customer

The first step to building a Product is to clearly identify the customer and the problem you are solving for the customer.

Knowing your customer will help you design the product right in such a way that the customer will find it easy and intuitive to us.

Is your customer a consumer? Then you have to make the product friendly with an informal tone of usage.

For example a Fitness band wearable shows a heart next to pulse rate and has a fun tone to the product flow on the device and in the mobile app. My Basis Peak fitness watch tells me to form habits for walking or sleeping for it to track my fitness habits. It cheers me when I wear the watch for 12 hours.

If your customer is an enterprise customer the tone of the design has to be formal. For example a product that tracks the temperature levels of a boiler will have to be formal and to the point to alert the customer as temperature levels begin to rise. It cannot have a funky tone and cheer on if the temperature comes down.

b. Is this customer tech savvy or not? This will help you decide how to simplify the setup of your product and ease of use. IoT products require setup to connect to the Internet that is easy for tech-savvy customers. If it is not a tech-savvy customer you will have to choose what connectivity you will use and decide on the setup that is easy and intuitive for the customer.

Look at an example such as the Amazon Dash, a consumer IoT product. Dash sets up Wi-Fi connectivity using a very easy on-boarding process for the average home consumer by utilizing their Mobile App to guide the setup process and pairing the device using the audio port on the Phone. So an average user has to download the Amazon Dash App and point the Dash device at their Mobile Phone. That's all.

2. Know your Customer's Market

For an IoT product the customer experience includes industrial design, user interface design with the various user flows and overall emotional hooks to engage the customer.

The type of industry this product operates in will dictate the privacy settings and any compliance requirements for the product. For example customers are very sensitive to healthcare information even beyond regulations to handle medical records in US. The European Union has a mandatory requirement for all cars to be equipped with eCall, an emergency smart car service that calls the nearest emergency center and sends minimum data including car location in the case of a collision.

These regulations dictate the level of storage of customer data and the presentation of compliance information to the customer as part of the customer experience.

The process of designing IoT Products becomes a two-way communication with customers more than any other product design process, because all IoT Products at their core collect data using sensors. For example, you can decide to create a product experience to tell the user about their ability to turn off storing of their behavioral data. But this customer flow might scare some users about the privacy of their data being collected and how you plan to use it. So it is important to design the customer flow at every step involving data to introduce them to the value they will derive from sharing data with you.

For example Kolibree the smart toothbrush collects data about a kid's brushing movements. It has woven this into the fabric of the product flow by making it into a mobile app the kid can play by brushing more. It then presents the data for a parent to see how well the kid is brushing her teeth. This way they earn the trust of the kid and the parent before they expose them to any flow asking for permission to store their data.

3. Know where Is the Value Created in Your Product

The critical piece unique to an IoT product different from any other technology product is to understand where is the value created in the product. Is it in the hardware, or connectivity or data? This value should be the pivot of the product experience to reinforce the value to the customer.

Even if it appears that there are many products similar to yours, if you know your customer and the value your product is creating for them, you can focus on the right product experience to create a unique product to earn the mindshare of your customer.

For a baby monitor the value is in alerting parents that the baby is awake using a Mobile App. The Mobile app interface where the parents get the alerts then becomes the key touch point to the customer to develop appreciation of the value created.

Where is the value created in Fitness Bands? Is it in the hardware that tracks the user's movements or in the data that presents the user's steps walked? If your customer is a normal walker, who wants to take charge of their health by walking daily towards their goals, then you create value in presenting their walking data relative to their goals. If your customer is someone stress prone needing to track their pulse rate to stay within healthy limits, the value is created in the hardware where the product shows the heart rate with a tiny heart symbol to give peace of mind to the customer.

CHAPTER 3 Building a new IoT Business

An IoT Product does not make a Business. A Product becomes a business when a set of customers get excited about it and engage with it to build it right, pay for its cost and in the case of the IoT Ecosystem, partner with the company to create a new market or category device.

PebbleBee team set out to invite the customer to join as beta testers for early shipping rewards right in their thank you announcement on reaching their Kickstarter goal. This set them for success to build the promised product into a successful business.

Figure 1: Thank You From PebbleBee Team

Intel and AWS hosted many hackathons where they gave out Intel Edison Boards to build out IoT Devices to connect to AWS Cloud. They partnered with the developers to understand how they use the boards, what were the gaps and how easy was it to use along with various sensors and what were the use cases for cloud usage specific to IoT. Intel has iterated to create a slew of boards and Amazon has created the AWS IoT product to meet the needs of the evolving IoT ecosystem led by the early developers shaping the space.

There will be many business decisions to be made along the way of building an IoT Business. They maybe about marketing methods, customer channels, issues in building the product as originally planned or unanticipated market adoption challenges.

None of these decisions have a single right answer. The important thing to remember is to always stay connected to your customer and be aware that these decisions shape not only the business you build but also the evolving IoT ecosystem.

3.1 Market Validating Your Product

The first step to building out your product into a business is to market validate that the customer need is real: that your product can solve the problem you promise.

Market validation for an IoT device is about getting who you believe to be your target customers to confirm that they are willing to pay money enough to cover the cost of making and distributing the IoT Product for them. In this early stage of the IoT ecosystem, market validation is being done using product prototypes because it costs substantial amount of money to build IoT device hardware with industrial design and to manufacture them in scale before they can be shipped to customers.

In Industrial IoT, products are optimizing existing process flows creating efficiencies. They are creating value by the real-time access to the data which various stakeholders would otherwise get access to in a month or few months time.

The process to build out the IIoT business starts with identifying a pilot that a company promises to build using sensors, data and dashboards. The customer agrees to pay for a Pilot program of the product. The product changes shape as it faces different hurdles of getting the various stakeholders of the product to change their old ways of operating. This adds to the risk of the business in proving its Return on Investment for its pilot. The company also has to source sensors cost effectively to build out the pilot, which introduces them to improving their own operations.

For example Smartly Solutions from Germany works with industrial clients to use Beacons to track factory stock of items during the production process. Prior to this there was no clear idea about the inventory of items available on the floor as they go through the production process and money was wastefully spent to order extra parts. In a pilot Smartly Solutions would select a section of a factory and setup beacons and provide the ROI of this IoT process improvement with real time dashboards.

For consumer products, entrepreneurs use crowd funding with Indiegogo or Kickstarter or other regional crowd fund platforms across the globe to market validate their products. A team conceives IoT devices and posts early prototypes and videos of the vision of finished products on Kickstarter to raise money from early adopters. This helps startups with seed funding and also validates the demand with early adopter customers.

Both consumer and industrial products have to iterate to create a market that scales. In the IoT ecosystem every customer creates new value from the product so sometimes it is just a matter of moving forward with many customer.

For example things.io an IoT cloud Platform keeps supporting a wide range of customers - a luggage tracker, a remote digital lock, digital thermometer, a smart fever tracker patch, a fashion jewelry wearable and more. With each customer they have iterated their product and reinforced the value they create to build out their business successfully.

3.2 Product Iterations to Meet Customer Demand

For a typical business, Iterative product design is about building out the actual product for the customer to get it, use it, and give feedback for you to iterate the product design to build the production version of the product that can be scaled to sell to many more customers.

An IoT Product design happens at hardware, Internet connectivity and software levels. So the IoT product design can be iterated in multiple layers of the product making it possible to design the same product in many different ways. These decisions will help you pivot your product to specific customer segments that will become your lifelong customers and impact the cost of building your product.

For example Nest thermostat includes a proximity sensor to detect movement of customers to decide if the customer is out of the house where they can turn down the heating. This is not typically part of smart thermostats. This adds to the total cost of making each Nest unit but comes with the unique customer luxury of forgetting to set the thermostat that you are away for heat savings to begin. In the crowded market of fitness bands Misfit has positioned itself as a fashion wearable focusing on the hardware design.

Sometimes the company is able to launch but not build the product cost effectively as the entrepreneurs had originally anticipated. This is when the team starts functioning as a company and learns operations. They also make decisions to keep the communication with their early customers that creates lasting customer trust and also gets them to set up what becomes core values of their business.

PebbleBee did a fantastic job of keeping up the customer communication at every step of the way with good and bad news and got their community of customers to go with them to build out their business.

Mini-Case study 1:

IoT Innovation: Item Finder

Business: PebbleBee

Product Innovation: PebbleBee built out a Bluetooth connected item finder that can locate items near an IOS or Android Phones.

Value from the Connected Device: Things ranging from bikes to keys to puppies can be located within the Bluetooth range near a mobile phone.

Business Value: The business value to the customer is in not losing important things. But PebbleBee shows the early adopters that it was building a quality product, cared about the customers to send them tested products and was going through challenges to build just the right Bluetooth locator product. This educated the early adopters, earned their trust away from similar sounding products from competition to stick with PebbleBee to help them build out their business successfully.

Lessons From PebbleBee's Market Development:

This case study is about how PebbleBee successfully engaged the original pledgers as beta users, kept up their communication as

---

they iterated and built out their product.

PebbleBee started with 3083 backers who pledged a total of $218,844 dollars in Feb 2014.

The PebbleBee team engaged the early customer community on Kickstarter and got input while sharing their successes and learning and had 2293 comments from the community as they stayed connected vested in getting PebbleBee to become a success.

PebbleBee team shared the first pictures of the products and built out excitement. They got feedback for the product brand name. They also shared their problems when they had to return the first batch of 200 to the manufacturers when they turned out that they were not class 1 quality buttons with 100,000+ clicks lifetime.

They shared their learning transparently with the community about broadcast cycles of the device with IPhones. IOS apps do not allow devices continuous access of Bluetooth connectivity to save Phone battery. This impacted how PebbleBee needed to always broadcast to the Phone costing more energy consumption.

Contrary to typical marketing practice about not telling the customer how a product is made, the PebbleBee team shared all details.

Figure 2 First version of PebbleBee

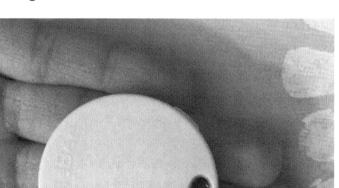

Image copyright: Sudha Jamthe

They shared their learning with honesty as they decided and iterated on plastic materials, texture, colors, PCB, assembly process and their ultrasound sealing procedure.

They patiently answered questions when customers asked them questions about their production decisions. Through all this they got the customers on their side convinced they were building a quality product. So when shipment delayed customers were sympathetic and showed their support.

Overall PebbleBee was able to deliver on their product. I even got a free replacement battery when their initial model drained faster than they had anticipated in their design.

Every step of the way the product got iterated. The customers stayed engaged and built trust with PebbleBee as it shaped up as a company improving their operations, customer support, brand loyalty and market scale to launch more product called PebbleBee Stone to extend their product line into the new market they created for themselves

3.3 Business Decisions to Shape Your Business

For an IoT Product that is a hardware device that promises to solve a specific problem it a challenge to switch to a totally different product and even more to get the initial customers to stay with the company as they shape themselves into a business.

Vessyl the hydration cup company faced that challenge, as they were unable to build the product they originally planned as they ran into consistency issues during product prototyping.

3.3.1 When you are unable to build the product as planned

Mini-Case study 2:

IoT Innovation: Hydration Cup

Business: Vessyl

Product Innovation: Vessyl set out to make a connected cup that will track all the fluids you drink to keep track of your hydration needs.

Value from the Connected Device: A connected cup that ensures you are correctly hydrated from all drinks from coffee to beer all through the day was a novel idea too good to be true.

Analysis of Vessyl's Market Development:

Vessyl set out to raise $50,000 but ended up raising $1Mil+ setup as a pre-sales campaign on its website in July 2014.

Vessyl created a buzz in the tech early adopter community because of its claim that you can pour any liquid into Vessyl cup and its advanced sensing technology will break down the fluid to a molecular level and instantly recognize the beverage type, caloric makeup, quantity and Pryme, what Vessyl team calls as optimal hydration levels.

Figure 3 Image Vessyl

Image: copyright Vessyl

The production of promised Vessyl got delayed. Vessyl team ran into technical hurdles to be able to consistently build a device that can break down any liquid.

This is a huge business risk because the early pre-order customers have a legal right to cancel their orders and get their money back.

Vessyl built a cup to measure water hydration levels easily similar to the product Water Glass that exists today. They have launched this water cup called as "Vessyl Pryme" and have emailed the early customers that they are giving Pryme which is a $99 value for free while they wait for the Vessyl cup as the company continues their research build the promised Vessyl.

But in the same email the company said, "As a heads up, once you opt in to receive a Pryme, your original Vessyl order becomes non-refundable." This is a strategy Vessyl team has taken to create a new product to check for water hydration levels and by giving it they absolve themselves of their commitment to deliver the Vessyl with its hard to crack challenges.

I do believe that the team must be continuing their research as promised for those who are patient to wait to support them.

Vessyl had failed to communicate to customers and build trust to understand their challenges, so customers were less likely to wait longer for the product. Instead Vessyl has made a business decision to extend their product line to a lower end product and by getting customers to absolve their right to cancel the Vessyl product they have chosen a path to reduce their business risk while retaining some of the customers and losing a lot of their early adopter customers.

3.3.2 When you cannot build a business standalone

You may face business decisions that will shape your new business. It could be about distribution channels, marketing, extending product lines, switching target customers to those who find real value from your product or changing the pricing model or partnerships or even exiting your company by merging into another company for better scale.

Mini-Case study 3:

IoT Innovation: Fitness Band for Fashion Industry

Business: Misfit

Product Innovation: Misfit created a fitness tracker similar to Fitbit, Jawbone, Xiaomi and many other wearables.

Value Creation: Misfit offers value of tracking the customer's health by tracking their fitness but also caters to the fashion sense of the customer.

Figure 4: Misfit Shine Fashion Fitness Wearable

Image: copyright Amazon

Lessons from Business Decisions:

Misfit could not scale their business with enough sales as a standalone business against Fitbit and Nike.

As the first step Misfit partnered with Speedo and Swarovski. This way it was able to target high end Fashion customers and differentiate itself as the Wearable Fitness market started getting crowded.

"If you don't have a brand, it is hard to be legit in this space," Sonny Vu, the co-founder and CEO of Misfit told *The Wall Street Journal.*

In Nov 2015 Misfit has exited by acquisition to The Fossil Group for $260Mil. Fossil Group sells 50 million watches per year and owns fashion brands Fossil and Skagen, and produces watched for brands Adidas, Emporio Armani, Michael Kors, Burberry, and DKNY.

By becoming a part of the Fossil Group, Misfit's technology has found a much broader audience as part of Fossil Group Watches by combining style with technology. Misfit is well poised to successfully create more fashion IoT products for Fossil Group Brands.

3.3.3 How to scale your own lead by innovating further

Mini-Case study 4:

IoT Innovation: Hardware Computer Boards to build IoT Products

Business: Raspberry Pi Foundation

Product Innovation: Raspberry Pi innovated to create a computer with Linux at the lowest market price of $5.

Lessons from Business Decisions:

Raspberry Pi makes computers to build IoT devices around $30 for a full computer that runs Linux and can be used to build IoT Devices. Given the proliferation of boards Raspberry Pi innovated ahead of its own self by creating a new computer called Raspberry Pi Zero at $5 that is the lowest price in the market.

Raspberry Pi has recently merged with Code Club an after school kids coding club with a mission to get a coding club in every community. So the $5 Raspberry Pi Zero is the perfect product extension for this audience and their new channel to school kids and hobbyists making Robots.

Raspberry Pi has done a brilliant marketing by embedding a Pi

Zero in every copy of the Nov 2015 edition of MagPi magazine.

Figure 5: Magpi magazine with Pi Zero

Image: copyright The MagPi

This is a business move to create a distribution channel with demand for its new product while communicating its size and low price to its target audience.

The Raspberry Pi has created a new lower end market by innovating ahead of its own existing product.

CHAPTER 4: Extend an Existing Business

All businesses are going to be impacted by IoT sooner or later. It is an excellent time for businesses to look at IoT as an opportunity before it becomes a threat and a new IoT business cannibalizes them.

Imagine a small business that offer swimming pool cleaning services. They are a localized service business and dependent on Yelp app or similar review sites to send them new business. They go clean a swimming pool and leave with some small change with no opportunity to build a relationship with their customer, not aware of when the customer would need their pool cleaned again. Now this business creates a small IoT product that checks the alkalinity of the pool and knows when the water needs to be cleaned and notify them. This takes a different set of skills to create an IoT product. They could even partner with or acquire a startup building such a product.

Then their whole business changes to one offering a small product to their customers the first time they service them. They can signup the customer for an annual service offering to come back proactively anytime their pool becomes dirty. First they get repeat business from their customers by switching from an on-call one off business to an annual service revenue. Next the pool cleaning company has the ability to collect data from multiple customers to understand their usage patterns and when the pools need cleaning. They can forecast customer demands to manage their business better. For example pHin in Palo Alto in US builds such an IoT pool cleaning product and is offering pool cleaning service that includes the IoT Product and Wi-Fi setup. This startup disrupts the space of pool cleaning service companies.

4.1 Partner with a Technology Company

Mini-Case study 5:

IoT Innovation: Connected Water Filter

Businesses: Brita in partnership with Amazon

Value from the Connected Device: Consumers do not have to suffer from forgetting to order refills for Brita water filters and can reorder by pushing a button to get Amazon delivery at their doorsteps.

Figure 6: Brita Filter Getting Refills with Amazon DRS

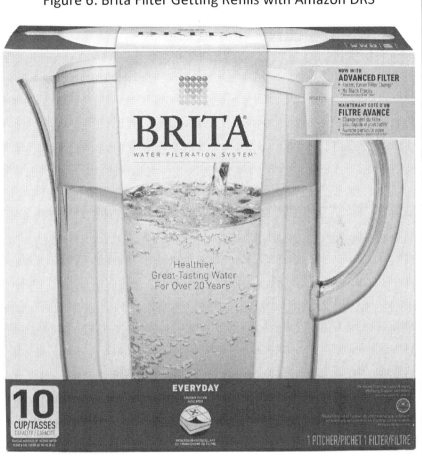

Product Innovation:

Amazon offers a Platform API for device manufacturers called "Dash Relinquishment Service" to connect to leverage Amazon's authentication and payment systems, customer service, and fulfillment network.

Brita plans to connect to Amazon's DRS service to seamlessly order water filter refills from Amazon by integrating the Dash Button into their appliance.

Business Value:

IoT creates wins with partnership across companies that bring different competencies to create an innovation ecosystem. This is a classic example of such partnerships that create value for both partnering companies and the customer.

Amazon has left control with manufacturers to decide if they want to build in an Amazon Dash like button in their device or bake the counting of usage and ordering refill automated inside the device so they can manage their own design for their brands while using DRS.

Brita is going beyond using the Dash button for refills but creating new value to customers by using the usage data of customers to understand their usage patterns to plan its inventory. Brita could potentially share this data with customers to create new value to help them stay hydrated similar to new IoT products such as Vessyl.

4.2 Develop Technology in-house

Mini-Case study 6:

IoT Innovation: Bluetooth Connected Pressure Monitor

Businesses: Omron

Value from the Connected Device:

A connected blood pressure monitor keeps tracks of blood pressure and heart rhythm trends using a mobile app making it easy for patients to see if there is something abnormal when they need to seek medical health.

Analysis of Extending the Business:

Omron is the top selling Blood pressure monitor on Amazon. Omron noticed smart watches and Fitbands track health vitals. They all measure pulse but Omron has the special technology to measure blood pressure.

Omron decided to extend its own product line with a Bluetooth connected version of its top selling Blood pressure monitor. It seamlessly upgraded itself with the existing brand and channels to sell the new connected Product without ever calling it an IoT. It offers a Mobile App to pair up with its device to track blood pressure trends and irregular heart beat.

Figure 7 Omron 10 Series Blood Pressure Monitor

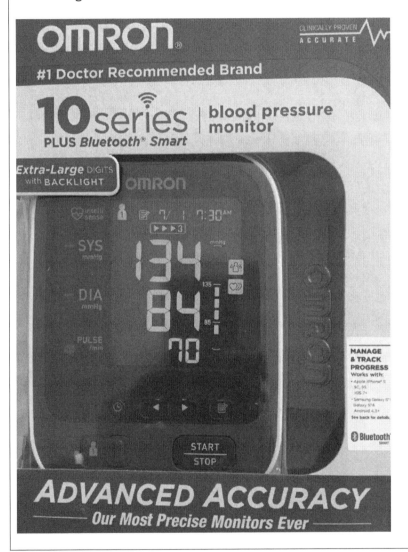

Omron has stayed focused on the value it offers to the customer who wants to check for their heart health and not the casual user looking to track their vitals out of curiosity.

Omron has built the next version of its product as a connected product well without playing defense to Fitness devices claiming the health conscious customer who are Omron's customers.

4.3 Keep Focus on your Core Brand

Mini-Case study 7:

IoT Innovation: Fitness Tracking for Athletes

Businesses: Nike

Lessons from Extending the Business:

In 2012, Nike launched a fitness band called Fuelband that successfully captured 10% of the fitness band users and built a community of runners around it. Then the market shifted with a proliferation of whole bunch of fitness bands driving the market growth.

Nike looked into its core business and realized it successfully sold shoes and helped athletes with shoes. It did not want to be pigeoned to be one of the fitness band players and compete in a crowded market. It stopped selling the fuelband device and instead decided to offer a digital fuelband app that supports any wearable. This strategy helped them focus on knowing and maintaining the relationship with the athlete with their existing shoes product line.

4.4 Be a Market Leader even as a Second Mover

Mini-Case study 8:

IoT Innovation: Connected Toothbrush

Businesses: Oral B

Value from the Connected Device: Offer data about brushing habit for dental hygiene.

Analysis of Oral B Extending its Business:

Oral B is a toothbrush maker. It offers a high-end automated toothbrush. IoT startup Kolibree has created a whole new value from a connected smart toothbrush by offering data for parents about how much time their kids brushed offering a fun game interface to engage kids to make brushing a fun family game.

Oral B has entered the connected toothbrush market to defend its business without a first mover advantage. Oral B's connected toothbrush is in early stages of customer experience development because it presents data from brushing without a consumable interface. Oral B has trusted channels with dentists and a loyal base of consumers who may not be game playing kids.

Oral B has to understand its own customer base in the broader toothbrush market to decide what unique value it is creating from its connected product and plan ahead instead of continuing to be follower in a new market.

4.5 Reach New Customer Segments

Mini-Case study 9:

IoT Innovation: Wireless speakers

Businesses: Harman/Kardon

Value from the Connected Device: Speakers can play music over the Internet remotely.

Harman the leader in high-end quality speakers has entered the connected speaker market by offering 8 Wi-Fi speaker products extending their existing business with connected products.

Figure 8 Harman/Kardon Wi-Fi speaker

Analysis of Extending the Business:

Harman has a loyal customer base that trusts their quality product. However for a wireless speaker the device's value cannot be communicated by itself to the average customer without showcasing what a connected wireless speaker can do.

Harman has begun engaging with the developer community to use Onyx their Wi-Fi speaker to give them feedback, to iterate and build out the product, the new market needs, with a supporting set of apps around it.

This is a bold move by Harman/Kardon to not only extend their product line but to begin building a relationship with a new set of user. With feedback from tech savvy developers Harmon/Kardon can build the right product and extend its business to the connected IoT space.

4.6 Collaborate to win New Markets

Mini-Case study 10:

IoT Innovation: Supercharger, a fast, connected car charger made by Tesla competing with slower chargers by BMW and Nissan each.

Businesses: BMW and Tesla

Analysis of Extending the Business:

Tesla made Supercharger a new electric vehicle charger which turned out to be superior to the chargers made by Nissan and BMW by offering faster charging in less time. Tesla started setting up charging stations around US while BMW was offering their charging stations for dealers to set up.

Nissan uses the CHAdeMO quick charge connector from Japan while BMW uses German-derived Combined Quick Charge Standard known as CCS. The incompatibility of different charges is fragmenting the electric vehicle market making it inconvenient to the customer, the electric car owner.

Tesla decided to open source its Electric Vehicle Technology Patents and open up Smart Charger standard for other car companies to operate on a joint agreement. BMW partnered with Tesla on this announcement and has agreed to use Tesla's Superchargers.

This is a good business move for Tesla to collaborate and open up its patents to allow for overall growth of electric vehicle market instead of being fragmented by few existing players.

This is a good business move by BMW to agree to collaborate on open standard for charging focusing on letting the customer win. This allows BMW and Tesla to focus on their core business to innovate and grow instead of competing on charging formats that is not core to their products or assets.

Chapter 5: The IoT Customer Experience

5.1 Why the Customer Experience is Important for IoT

IoT Products make our life simpler but they require us to adopt new behaviors or unlearn old habits. For example it will take me a long time to walk away from my home knowing that my smart lock will lock my home when I leave. Customer experience is how we engage with a product to use it. Good customer experience is very important in an IoT Product because the product has the responsibility to inspire users to change their behavior to derive the best possible value.

A fitness wearable can track my health vitals but if I ignore abnormal values I will not benefit from it.

5.2 Operations Behind Customer Experience

How would you feel about a brand or product if you follow through a notification they send on your mobile but it leaves you with an incomplete customer experience?

Target in Sunnyvale, California has a Starbucks inside it. When I drive to the Target, right at the parking lot I get a notification from the Target App offering a Starbucks Coupon.

Yes, I would love a coupon from Starbucks. So I go to the Target store and click on the notification from my Phone and it opens the Target App. The Target app has no recollection of offering me any Starbucks coupon. So my customer experience ends in a dead end.

The Starbucks inside the Target store is a partnership and they each have their own Mobile Apps. It appears that the customer flow connecting the geo fencing notification does not have any operational backend to really execute on giving me, the customer, the promised coupon for Starbucks. I am a fan of both Starbucks and Target, so I hope they fix this quickly.

This is a critical lesson that IoT customer experience is not just about partnerships or building beautiful devices. It is what your customer experiences whether it comes from you or a partner or your connection to another company's product or service. Offering a seamless customer journey in IoT is a challenge today because the customer journey is connected to different companies and applications that do not build upon the same technology.

5.3 End to End IoT Customer Experience

The end-to-end customer experience of an IoT Product spans the hardware and software. It has five customer touch points where a Product Manager has to make decisions to offer the best customer experience.

1. Industrial Design: An Internet of Thing consists of the hardware that requires good industrial design to make it usable for the target customer. I would include the necessary communication of feature/benefit from packaging to this customer touch point.

Bass Peak offers a Fitness Smart Watch. Their packaging eloquently places the watch in an appealing box and communicates the features and value in the package.

2. Customer Onboarding or Setup: Having a good Customer Experience when setting up an IoT product is a huge hurdle for non-tech users because it typically requires registration not only of the user's identity but also requires the device to be setup to

be connected to the Internet.

3. Connectivity Choices

All IoT devices collect data and usually send it to the cloud for processing. So it is important to understand how intensive the bandwidth and throughput payload of the data is and choose the right connectivity to the Internet. Otherwise wait time delays can communicate a bad customer experience with the product and likely lose the customer.

4. Presentation of Value from Data

The data transmitted by the IoT device should be presented in a way that it inspires the customer to take the necessary action to consume the value. For example let us take Kolibree smart toothbrush. The data showing how well your kid brushes her teeth was not previously collected or exposed to us. This creates value for the customer not just in seeing this data but also in getting kids to brush often and well.

Kolibree offers the best example of a consumer IoT data presentation that inspires its users. It offers a mobile app for users to move ahead by brushing with the Kolibree toothbrush. This encourages the kid to keep brushing and helps parents see their brushing patterns.

Figure 9 Kolibree Smart Toothbrush App

Image Copyright Kolibree

5. <u>Mobile App User Interface:</u> The final part of an IoT product is the mobile app, which sends notifications. This is the most common touch point of the user to keep them engaged and using the product. So this needs to be a simple, intuitive UI that connects with the user containing the right emotional hooks.

The Amazon Dash Button is the 1-click IoT button a user can press to order refills for consumables such as soap or pet food. I had my Dash Button connected to Tide laundry detergent. I pressed a button and Amazon registered a transaction to send me a box of Tide. As a cool new toy in our home, of course, we played with it and did demos to visitors of our home causing repeat orders. Amazon has found a way to deal with this and gives us the option to quickly cancel repeat orders from the Dash App.

6. The Core Experience in Hardware vs. Software

A customer does not experience an IoT device only in the industrial design of the slick cool device with smooth edges, or the software setup and mobile app interface. Good IoT customer experience resides in the thoughtful implementation of many use cases designed to accommodate how the customer will use the product at any given time.

A product manager should have empathy and intuition to think of ways a customer will try to use an IoT product. If you expect them to solve a particular problem using the hardware, be open to collect data and adapt the product if you find that the user is using more of the software part of the IoT.

Alarm.com home security system is a classic example of good IoT customer experience that spans multi-device interface and offers many uses with a fanatic focus on customer's security.

Full Case study 11:

IoT Innovation: Connected Security Alarm for Home

Business: Alarm.com Home Security Alarm

Value from Connected Device: Alarm.com gives peace of mind to monitor the home for a break-in and remotely track the status of open doors and windows.

Strategic Product Design Analysis:

Alarm has many more use cases that is strategically built into the product design. Alarm can be armed or disarmed remotely using a mobile app or a hardware wall mount unit or a hardware keychain.

The Alarm.com has two hardware pieces, a wall mounted unit and a keychain.

The Wall unit is connected using a Phone line that keeps it always connected even if the home Wi-Fi is down. They can also press and call a support service in case of an emergency. If the burglar alarm goes off in an emergency situation, an on-call person calls from this unit to check on the situation or call the Police.

The Mobile app is intuitive to use. We can setup a security password for each person with his or her own logins and notification alerts. The app presents a view to show status of all sensors of the home. An additional notification view in the mobile app offers an additional use case to check who opened or closed a particular door and when a bypassed sensor was armed again. I know of parents who look for this notification from their babysitter opening and closing their front doors at specific times after they pick up their kids to signal that their kid is now safe at home.

Figure 10 Alarm.com Security system mobile app screenshot

Image Copyright Sudha Jamthe

Product Design Towards Good Security:

Alarm.com keychain is the main control that identifies the owner of the security system. If a user lost the security keychain they can change passwords on the Apps and it synced with the home security system. But there was no way to disconnect the lost hardware keychain from our home security system. It is not clear if Alarm.com is catering to some security use case by creating this point of user identity tied to the keychain.

Alarm.com security alarm offers a brilliant multi-device product design of a rare but useful security use case. If the user leaves a patio door open and forgets about it and tries to arm the house with the keychain, the main unit in the wall will arm the house but scream that the door is open till the user verifies their identity by entering their password and disarms and arms the house from the wall unit. This protects the user from the rare case if some intruder has entered the house through the open door and the user is using the keychain to arm the house to lock up all other doors and windows. In this case all other doors and windows are armed and if the intruder opens any door it will start the security alarm and call the police.

Security issues typically creep up in the customer experience in the gap between the hardware and software touch points of an IoT product. Alarm.com has taken good care to maintain security while managing customer use of product from multiple interfaces.

5.4 Partnerships and IoT Customer Experience

The Internet of Things ecosystem has been bringing a constant flow of partnerships by companies to provide interoperability or better portfolio of products for customers.

September 2015 saw an interesting set of IoT Partnership announcements.

IBM and ARM announced their collaboration to offer an end-to-end solution that goes from chipset to the cloud services for IoT Product builders. ARM licenses 1 Billion chips per quarter for Internet of Things Devices and is building an IoT operating system called mBed. This partnership allows anyone using ARM chip for mBed IoT devices access to IBM's Bluemix.

Apple, Boeing and Pentagon formed the Flex Alliance to create flexible 3D printed wearable for the US Army, creating the Flexible Hybrid Electronics Manufacturing Innovation Hub in San Jose, CA. This brings Boeing and Apple together to create new wearable products for the US Army.

Blackberry bought Good Technologies in Sept. 2015 for $425 Million in cash. Analyst Ray Wang says (I paraphrase Ray here) that with Good technology's Product suite with 70+ security certificates Blackberry can now build an Internet of Things Platform for the Enterprise across iOS and Android.

IoT Product and Business managers need to think about partnerships as an opportunity to enhance the customer value. Partnerships are important particularly in IoT because a single IoT spans a variety of technology interfaces with many players developing expertise in different parts of IoT.

In a partnership it is important to have clarity and communicate to the customer who owns which part of the customer relationship. Both companies in such partnerships should work together to design an integrated customer experience without fragmenting the customer experience between their two products.

The IoT Product setup should offer an integrated experience. If each partner has different software, it is important to ensure that they are interoperable and do not cause any confusion to the user on using specific versions of their products for their combined use.

The customer will purchase the product or service from one brand and will expect them to solve all their problems. For example if a IoT maker builds a new product using ARM chips and uses IBM Bluemix for analytics, if they run into any issues, both ARM and IBM should be prepared to help the customer without pointing them to the other company.

5.5 Multi-Device Customer Experience

IoT as a product spans across hardware, mobile app and any interface to other systems. This adds complexity to offer multi-device or multiscreen experiences.

Michal Levin's book "Designing Multi-Device Experiences" is a good multiscreen design guide for mobile, which is equally extendable to connected devices. Micah Levin says multi-screen experiences can be designed in three possible methods. These are consistent, complementary or continuous experience from one customer touch point to another.

Figure 11a and 11b Nest Image Device and Nest App

Image Copyright Sudha Jamthe   Image Public domain

Nest Labs was co-founded by Apple engineers Tony Fadell and Matt Rogers in 2010 with a vision to create connected home automation products. Its products include Nest Learning Thermostat, Nest Protect Smoke detector and Nest Cam security camera. Google acquired Nest for $3.2 billion in cash in January 2014. Nest has split from Google Inc. and is now part of Alphabet Inc. as part of their corporate restructuring in August 2015.

The Nest Thermostat is a good example of an IoT device that offers a consistent multi-screen experience between its hardware and software touch points. It presents a very clean, easy to use industrial design for a connected thermostat and reflects the same in its mobile app. Look at the picture and you can see that the actual device and app look exactly the same. They can be used the same way too. You can turn the aluminum ring cover of the nest device and push it to set the temperature or do the same on the App and it syncs seamlessly between the two.

Matt Rogers co-founder of Nest Labs said in 2011 at the launch of the first version of the Nest Thermostat, "It's about saving money, saving energy, but it's also about a product that is beautiful. Something you appreciate having on your wall".

Nest calls itself a learning system, uses machine learning and tries to learn the user's temperature setting preferences to set the temperature by itself. Nest faces the problem of home automation products where the product has multiple customers. This creates a challenge in being able to truly learn the preferred setting for the family when different members of the same house prefer different temperature settings. This data can mislead the learning system. Nest Thermostat clearly offers customers energy savings. It shares it transparently with their energy history feature. But with Nest now having a series of home automation products, Nest Cam security camera that is always on, Nest Protect smoke detector all talking to each other, customer have begun speculating what data Nest collects and what it will do with it.

This is a common problem for IoT products used by consumers. Product Managers have to earn the trust of the customer by showing value from the data collected and then give user the option to turn of sharing such data.

Most Home automation products such as Philips Hue light, home security Alarm, motion sensors, security cams, water hydration systems, pet feeders all offer a complementary experience. You can use the actual device to do the function of the product and the mobile app to check on the status or next step action. For example, with the home security Alarm you could arm it using the keychain and use the app to check that all doors are closed as a continuous experience.

A complementary experience is one where you can do one action on one device and the next step on another screen. Something akin to "Watch with eBay" where you are watching a TV show and using your iPad to order the show's branded items at the same time.

Complementary experiences across multiple touch points for an IoT Product are not common.

Maybe you will apply a complementary experience for your product as you build your next business successfully.

Part II: Internet of Things Applications

"Wearables and the IoT are rapidly altering the landscape of everyday life, fashioning innovative paths to wellness, productivity, and creativity. Wearables and the IoT are affecting more than step counts and heart rates—-every industry is being changed through the use of the information gathered from IoT devices and sensors." - **Scott Amyx, CEO Amyx McKinsey and Wearable and IoT Thought Leader**

CHAPTER 6: Wearables and Quantified Self

Wearables are IoT Products worn by babies, adults, seniors and pets. These typically include fitbands, watches, health sensors, and devices embedded in clothing and accessories that we wear on ourselves. Wearable applications are exploding as they tap into consumer pains and passions left unsolved by the Internet by creating value from the data from the always-on connectivity.

6.1 Quantified Self

Quantified self refers to the movement where we collect and analyze data about our bodies. Quantified self makes us willingly put our life under scrutiny by IoT devices watching did we sleep well, brush our teeth the right way, eat the right kind of foods, are we hydrated, what are our health vitals, are we in danger and do we need to call for help and whether we are sleeping, breathing and exercising for optimal living.

New wearables coming up daily add a new set of biometrics that was not collected before. We have IoT devices that track our cortisol level in our brains, bacteria in our gut and insulin levels in our blood giving us the ability to quantify our vitals and to help us manage our lives with awareness and live longer.

Mini-Case study 12:

Figure 12 Google Contact Lens

Image Copyright Google Inc.

IoT Innovation: Blood Glucose Monitoring Contact Lens

Business: Google & Novartis

Product Innovation: Google has partnered with Novartis to make blood glucose level monitoring for people using contact lenses. Google X life sciences team has invented and patented this technology but partnered with Novartis, the contact lens manufacturer to build this.

Value from the Connected Device: This is an innovation that frees diabetic people from having to poke their fingers to draw blood to test for blood glucose levels. Also it frees this testing from being dependent on the human to do it at random times and automates it.

Business Value: Novartis gets to extend its business to the new world of IoT with technology license from Google X and continue its core competency of building contact lens. Also Novartis owns the customers who buy contact lens in terms of channels and their trust. So Novartis can distribute the early version of the lens and Google can get customer feedback to iterate to build this product right to meet the needs of its diabetic consumers.

6.2 Fitbands, Smart Watches and Flying Cameras

The categories of wearables can be exhaustive, but most are positioned into Fitbands and Smart Watches. In the future, wearable flying cameras may be a segment onto itself.

Fitbit, Jawbone and a slew of health fitness bands created the market for wearables because they created a simple customer experience and focused on the passion of users to take charge of their longevity by measuring their daily steps. They motivated customers to wear their fitness band and track their steps for walking or running. Some user interfaces were very simple and did not offer a display but offered a companion App on the smart phones thereby reducing the cost of the device.

These wearable bands rode the social sharing bandwagon and scales adoption. Soon the market got fragmented with many fitness band wearables in a wide price range.

Figure 13 Wearable Smart Watch Basis Peak

Image Copyright Sudha Jamthe

Smart Watches As a New Device Category

The Idea of a Smart Watch that could do more than just tell time helped create a new category of device Smart Watches were not the first wearables to be introduced to consumers but they were the first to be accepted by consumers. They garnered a tremendous amount of venture funding, creation of new companies, and media coverage.

Smart watches are forecast to sell 25 Million units worldwide by end 2015.

Hybrid Fitness Band and Smart Watch

The Withings Activate, Basis Peak all look like classic watches but act like a fit band, an important factor driving their adoption. They track steps, sleep and health vitals but do not offer additional apps by other developers. This category is growing led the customer experience and increasing feature set of these devices.

Smart Watches Similarity and Difference with Fitness Bands

Smart Watches have created a whole new category of devices that are like wearable fitness bands and also smart devices like a smart phone. They track fitness health details but also come with apps offering a range of options. Many App developers who have their apps on the phones have offered extensions of their apps to send notification on the Apple Watch or Google Gear Watches. This assumes that the user of a Smartphone is the same as the Smart Watch in their behavior and need to use either of these devices. This is not the case as the Smart Watch is not cannibalizing Smart Phones and is growing as its own category.

As the market for Smart Watch matures we will have enough data to understand the behavioral difference between the users to design products different for Mobile from the Smart Phone. Apple initially tied the Apple Watch Apps to the iPhone and has now separated them out allowing for developers to create original Apps for the Apple Watch. For example eBay App sends notification to Apple Watch or Google Gear when a user's bid is outbid.

Smart Watches and Fitness bands are driving the Quantified self movement getting consumers ready to learn about health data to take charge of what their lifestyles.

Maybe you will figure out whole new products to make the Smart Watch attain its optimal business value for the customer.

Mini-Case study 13:

IoT Innovation: Fitness Band with GPS from Garmin

Business: Garmin

Product Innovation: Garmin has been a market leader in GPS systems. It has introduced two well-accepted models of fitness band wearables called Vivoactive and Forerunner that have incorporated GPS into a fitness band.

Value from Connected Device:

Garmin GPS tracks running, cycling, walking and swimming with the accuracy of a GPS system and is positioned as the perfect watch for the sports athlete. It even offers Golf tracking with built in 38,000 golf courses it can track using its GPS system.

Business Value: Garmin has extended it product lines to new IoT Products built upon its core expertise of making GPS systems and offers it as an additional offering to its existing base of sports athletic consumer.

One could look at Garmin's move as a defensive move to enter the connected devices space because Iot impacts city traffic tracking and location sensors are coming up in many IoT Products. But I see Garmin as a good example of an established business becoming nimble to use its expertise to enter a new market.

Enter Nixie the Flying Camera!

Nixie is a wearable flying selfie camera. That says it all. It is changing the future of photos by capturing the moment because it flies as it snaps a picture.

Nixie is an example of how a wearable does not have to be a fitness device or a watch running lots of apps and the world of wearable is open to unlimited possibilities.

What if you had a wearable that you could unleash and it could quickly vacuum the room or walk your dog and one that could check for CO levels to tell a worker it is safe to enter a mine. This in my imagination inspired by Nixie.

Maybe you will go build these some day.

6.3 Wearable Clothes – T-Shirt, Socks, Shoes, Bra

Wearables now come in discrete form embedded in clothing. Wearable manufacturers find or build sensors that are washable, iron proof and so discreet in size that they do not poke people on their clothing.

Ralph Lauren has a wearable T-Shirt that tracks the sweat level of the user. Sensoria fitness has an embedded heart rate monitor inside T-shirts and Bras. Many shoes come with sensors to track the movement of users. Sensoria fitness has a wearable sock that is infused with their proprietary textile sensors that tracks the running pattern of users and advises them on good running posture for their feet. This is a huge product innovation because it involves making sense of the data patterns from a user's running to make recommendations about optimal placement of their feet during running.

Figure 14 Sensoria Wearable Sock

Image Copyright Sudha Jamthe.

Wearables are being tested in the realm of Fashion. There are many wearable bracelets and Jewelry out there that blink with lights and do fun things.

Wearables are also driving the new field of Digital Health in with amazing medical Informatics and convenience to detect diseases and improve our life expectancy.

6.4 Consumers Different from Customers

The distinction between the consumer and the customer is important to keep in mind as you read through this section because they have product design and usability implications. You have to design for the consumer to find it useful and inspiring to keep using the product while you design for the customer to derive value from the product enough to pay for it.

6.4.1 Peace of mind for Pet owners

I tried to add a Gimbal low power BLE sensor on our puppy's collar so she could be tracked and we can keep her safe. She chewed on it within a day and immobilized it. Today there are many proximity sensors that are available to track pets, or any items from getting lost. *So there is a challenge to solve in designing a pet tracker product that works not just for the human customer but also for the consumer, the pet.*

Wearables for pets protect pets within a perimeter and inform the parent that the pets are safe. Pet owners are beginning to use Iot Products to keep their pets safe and also take care of them remotely when they are away.

We use a remote Wi-Fi enabled camera to watch our puppy remotely and an Amazon Dash button that offers 1-click ordering of consumables to re-order pet food when it depletes.

Some pet owners who have multiple pets use RFID sensors on Pet doors to separate feeding of two pets. Pet feeders is a fast growing Connected Product that dispenses food for pets be it fishes or cats and dogs. It is not a surprise because it is easy to use and gives peace of mind to pet owners who are busy and want to keep their pets well fed and safe.

Pets in America have had embedded chips in them for many years. This is not a connected device but pet shelters use a specialized reader to read these chips to locate the pet's family if they get lost.

Figure 15 Dog with Pet Tracker Wearable

Image Copyright Sudha Jamthe

6.4.2 Helping Parents Keep kids Safe

These set of products that are used by babies provide peace of mind to the parent that their babies are safe without any risk of human error.

Intel has a baby car seat that can check if baby is fastened correctly or else alert parents before a child gets hurt. Connected Baby monitors allow babies to be monitored by Parents and caretakers remotely. A baby diaper checks for wetness and notifies the parent.

Proximity sensors have many different applications for baby safety different from their use case in Retail environment. Filip, Tinitell, HereO are wearable GPS phones for little kids that Moms can use to monitor kids in playground within a certain vicinity. These solve the problem of notifying parents when kids go out of certain distance comfortably accepted by parents.

6.4.3 Wearables For Animal Conservation

Sarah Eccleston works as Director IoE (Internet of Everything as Cisco calls it) in Ireland and is passionate about connected cars and connected homes, and wanted to extend it to connected cows and connected elephants.

Wait, this is not a joke. But real passion is at work here.

This is the story of the human spirit and perseverance of one woman to learn, adapt and contribute to her passion.

Figure 16 Sarah Saved Elephants with IoT Trackers

Image Copyright Sarah Eccleston

An elephant gets killed for ivory every 15 minutes. Sarah wondered whether an IoT sensor on an elephant and track its biometrics to save it. She could not save elephants but she saved the elephant babies if they could know when an elephant mother was attacked. If they could get this information in real-time they could catch poachers and save future elephant from being killed by the poacher.

Sarah applied to Game Rangers International elephant orphanage in Zambia. She spent one month in Kalule as a researcher. The elephant orphanage is for baby elephants saved after a ruthless poacher kills the mother elephant. People have no way of finding out that an elephant was killed. They cannot save elephant babies unless somehow they can track the elephant's location and get a notification as soon as it is attacked and is dying.

Stop for a minute and join me in reading the rest of this story in context. Sarah works in High Tech in Ireland and like you and me she must have only seen elephants in a Zoo. Maybe she petted one some day too. She is not an animal trainer. Maybe like me she feels scared by the size of an African Wild Elephant. Or maybe not!

Sarah volunteered her way to a camp in Zambia in the wild with no electricity and running water. First she set out to build a solar powered Wireless LAN network and setup Internet connectivity in the middle of the remote jungle.

Sarah soaked in the knowledge of the anti poaching staff. She learned to identify elephants in the wild and the process the staff followed to help with conservation.

She put IoT sensors on elephants. When an elephant is shot its biometrics are sent to the rangers who could rush to the location and save the elephant if it is not too late. Thanks to Sarah they were even able to confiscate weapons and catch some poachers too.

Join me in drawing inspiration from imagining the picture of Sarah smiling when she saves an elephant.

Maybe you will build wearables for conservation of more animals.

CHAPTER 7: Connected Home or Smart Home

Connected Home or Smart Home makes our home appliances smart and creates new conveniences and solves for frustrations that we have learned to live with.

There are many fun products for the connected home but we will focus on the customer experience of connected home products and the unique opportunities and challenges they pose for entrepreneurs and product managers to build out IoT businesses.

Connected Home products are evolving in three areas focusing on different pain points of the home consumer.

7.1 Energy Efficiency From Connected Products

One set of connected products focus on energy efficiency. These products reduce energy consumption of our home appliances by turning them off when we are away and turning them on exactly when we enter our home or when we need them. This includes our thermostats, lights, Air Conditioner, and many electrical appliances such as toasters, dishwasher, fridge etc.

As a product designer the challenge in building such products lies in being able to communicate the value of the energy saving with simple consumer interfaces. Nest Thermostats is the market leader of this category. It provides a learning mode offering to learn a user's temperature setting behaviors so it can set the optimal temperature for a home without bothering the user to keep setting different temperature setting for different seasons, days and time of the day.

This poses interesting design problems because a home thermostat is not a personal device and will be used by many different users in the same home. How do you design a new product for a multi-customer experience? Also early adopter users tend to play with the thermostat to try different settings misleading the learning system on what is the real temperature desired by the customer. How do you teach the learning system what is real data and what is noise from exuberant new users?

Mini-Case study 14:

IoT Innovation: A Connected Light Bulb

Innovator: Philips Lighting (part of Koninklijke Philips N.V.)

Value from A Connected Device:

The light bulb is a simple product that provides light by turning on a switch. By turning it into a connected product the light can now be turned on or off remotely, to a programmed schedule and to other devices for gesture or voice control.

Business Value:

Philips has been innovating in making the light bulb more energy efficient. But now the company has created a whole new competency of a connected product able to talk to the Internet with an open software layer. Philips has also shown amazing agility by integrating with other new startups shaping the IoT space such as Octoblu and Home Automation hubs. This has helped Philips create more value for the connected customer and establish Philips as the first mover in a new connected light market.

This connected light bulb has helped Philips expand from a

connected home product to connected city lighting and Retail Lighting offering new value to a new set of customers expanding to whole new markets.

Figure 17 Philips Hue Bulb at work at Target Open House, a Demo Smart Home in San Francisco

Image Copyright Sudha Jamthe

The second set of connected products focuses on creating new conveniences by making everything in our home connected to the Internet and to each other.

This covers our smart garages, smart locks, gesture or voice controlled smart lights and garden watering systems solving for problems that we didn't even dream were solvable.

These connected home products replace existing not-so- smart devices. For a new startup that builds these devices it is a challenge to procure the distribution channels and acquire new customer relationships. Also the startups have to bear the brunt of educating customers about the new value from connecting devices that were not connected before motivating them to change their behavior into using the products differently. On the other hand, established businesses that own the customer relations with unconnected products will be cannibalized if they don't adopt by becoming connected devices. They will have to develop a whole new skillset of adding Internet connectivity, creating software layers and offering services to customers from their old model of selling a hardware product through established retail channels.

7.2 Connected Home Entertainment

The third set focuses on smart home entertainment. Connected Home entertainment is in infancy offering incremental innovations to the old worlds of home entertainment. This one focuses on changing our TV to become smart, connected to our mobiles and streaming digital devices.

There are a whole class of connected entertainment products evolving that make incremental shifts to functionality of Home entertainment systems operated by Gesture control or voice activated and speakers that are Wi-Fi enabled.

Consumers have to choose between creating an iPhone or Android home today with many fragmented new IoT devices from new startups adding small conveniences.

This area is ripe for the entrepreneur to create an integrated customer experience that wows the customer with seamless digital entertainment that taps into their desire to socialize with friends, family gatherings in the safety of their homes and seamlessly extending their digital mobile lives to their homes.

Maybe you will innovate a whole new world of home entertainment in the connected world of the future.

7.3 Fragmented Connected Home Experience

If you want to turn on your lights at specific times when you enter your home or adjust your blinds to sunrise, IoT Products exist to help you but there are too many devices not compatible with each other. Home devices today do not talk to each other leaving the consumer confused about what device is compatible with others.

Lack of Open Connectivity Standards

There are many competing open connectivity standards evolving as device makers are still figuring out details about privacy and security of devices connecting to each other.

AllJoyn and Thread are Open standard at a chip level for Connected Home. Weave is a new standard at the Mesh network level focused on security. There are many standards at the IP software level.

It is a challenge for the product developer to figure out what open standards to adhere to for their new IoT Product so many are choosing to offer standalone products that do not fit into any standard.

"Companies that connect to others to create value for the customer from integrated products will be the winners of the Connected Home space" says Jürgen Wege founder of AALIOT, an open source hardware project.

Hub Model

Existing companies such as Philips, Sharp and Belkin have jumped into the foray modifying their proprietary remote and hub systems to become Internet savvy but still keeping their proprietary communication between their remote and hubs. Wink/Iris are two Home Automation hubs that connect to two different sets of competing devices and sold by the two competing US Home Supply retailers Home Depot and Lowes respectively.

Hubs also become the single point of failure for the entire connected home. They also make it complex for customers to figure out what device to buy based on what Hub they have invested in already. This area is ripe to find a non-Hub based solution such as provided by Yonomi or to create products such as anythings.co that help customers figure out what are the connected use cases and what product is compatible to another.

Mini-Case study 15:

IoT Innovation: Wink Home Automation Hub

Business: Quirky

Value from the Connected Device: The hub connected disparate devices to work together in a home acting as the central point of connectivity for these devices.

Business Case:

Quirky has been an innovative New York based startup well respected by the IoT early adopter community. Quirky raised $185.3Million in 8 rounds of funding.

Quirky successfully got a distribution for Wink, its flagship Home Automation Hub Product with the US Retailer Home Depot. But Wink could not scale as expected so Quirky sold Wink to Flextronics and declared Chapter 11 Bankruptcy in Sep 2015.

Reasons for Wink's failure:

Wink bore the brunt of educating the market as one of the first movers.

It had difficulty to get adoption with non-tech users because the setup was complicated because of incompatibilities of the IoT home products.

Wink could not get Home Depot sales team trained and incentivized to sell enough of its product in scale.

App Fatigue

Today each Connected Home Product comes with its own Mobile App for customers to get notifications and operate the device remotely. With the fragmented market this has led to customer needing 10 to 20 apps to manage their homes.

I believe that the company that offers the most easy to use simple customer experience for mainstream consumers with unrivaled service will become the undisputed market leader of the connected home space.

CHAPTER 8: Connected Cars and Flying Drones

Cars have begun becoming smart with Internet connectivity and in most cases it is not even marketed to the average car buyer. Tesla has been the unrivaled leader of the connected car space. In Nov 2015 Tesla introduced their Autopilot mode for the S Series making it a self-driving car in a limited sense with a simple over the air software update to the cars.

Millions of cars today have MirrorLink, an open standard to connect Cars, Smart Phone and Consumer Electronic devices in cars. However many global car manufacturers have created Automobile Innovation centers in Silicon Valley to work with Apple and Google to get their Google Android Auto and Apple CarPlay integrated into their cars to provide smartphone connectivity to both Android and iPhones respectively.

Beyond the carmakers and Apple and Google, there are so many product innovations that are coming up daily and many more waiting for you my readers.

As you join me in this chapter think of this not as a connected car space but as modern transportation in a connected world.

Figure 18 Tesla Smart Car Chassis

Image Copyright Sudha Jamthe

8.1 Self Driving Cars

Robots have been used in industrial setting for a long time to transport things across machine floors. Self driving cars have build on this innovation to create a Robot that can learn driving in a consumer setting. Did you know that self-driving cars just do not learn road rules? Instead they have been introduced scenarios such a golf cart crossing their path to allow them to learn what they need to learn to understand human traffic patterns using Machine Learning Algorithms.

Self driving cars are not an innovation only for the road but impact reducing the number of drivers, freeing up parking space in cities and the potential introduction of self-driving vehicles in other areas of life and in the air.

So this impacts urban planning and takes us to a new world where consumers riding self-driving cars will need whole different products and product experiences in the not too distant future.

8.2 Self Servicing Cars

A connected car can track the health and safety of the vehicle from the data it collects and monitors in real time.

8.2.1 Cars Calling for Emergency Help

European Union has a mandatory requirement for all calls to be equipped with eCall, an emergency smart car service that calls the nearest emergency center and sends minimum data including car location in the case of a collision. This has sped up smart car deployments in Europe.

8.2.2 Car Telematics for Routine Maintenance

Telematics

Cars send vehicle diagnostics to the dealer offering fleet maintenance proactively and offer entertainment, weather, and traffic information on our cars. Tesla Motors is the undisputed market leader in connected cars. Tesla is leading the way for other car manufacturers on smart car features and Telematics that can be incorporated adding value to customers.

8.2.3 OTA – Over the Air Update

OTA or Over The Air update for cars is an area of technology development that is growing actively. The operating system in the Tesla car is remotely updated similar to an Apple Phone OS update without the need to visit the dealer. This is what Tesla used to update the Model S cars with an Autopilot feature. Movimento is evolving as the leader in OTA services for cars. Some car manufacturers are opting to provide basic apps with the cars while others plan to update Apps using wireless networks to keep the apps up to date in cars. Continental, Denso, Ford, GM, Jaguar Land Rover, Panasonic, Shanghai GM, and Volvo cars all provide Over the Air updates using Movimento.

8.2.4 Business Questions about Car Connectivity

Connectivity: The connected car needs a wireless service to communicate with the Internet. This is posing a challenge because consumers are used to paying a one-time purchase price for a car while connected car services will require monthly payments like a Phone service. Nissan's Leaf EV cars come with AT&T 2G network paid for by Nissan. When AT&T expires the 2G network in 2017, the car's connection will stop working unless upgraded to a 3G network. The verdict is out on who will bear the cost of the connectivity of connected cars and how this will play out as a business model in car sales.

Tesla uses an automotive development platform from AT&T and does not charge customers separately for the monthly connectivity costs.

Security: Cars come with mechanical, electronic and electrical parts. Software and data connectivity over the cloud and wireless access are not a core competency for car manufacturers.

This lack of expertise has led to cases where car software had critical security gaps. This needs to be carefully crafted, as it is a critical component of the connected car customer experience.

Charlie Miller and Chris Valasek spent three years researching to find a security issue in Chrysler Jeeps. They made news when they demonstrated live to Wired Magazine writer Andy Greenberg that they could take over and paralyze his Jeep while he was driving it. Chrysler responded and mailed a security patch software in USB sticks to 1.4 million customers because the car was not setup to do an Over The Air update.

Fleet management and Insurance companies with usage based insurance give drivers a 2-inch dongle device to plug into a car's dashboard to collect location and driving data. Researchers at Usenix conference in August 2015 have demonstrated that these dongle devices have security vulnerabilities that can allow hackers to cross the gap between a car's cellular-connected infotainment system and its steering and brakes. TomTom's Coordina, Metromile Pulse from Mobile Devices of France, Progressive's Snapshop, the dongle vendors have responded with fixes.

This raises the bar for product managers of all devices and systems that can connect to a car to become more aware of security issues and design products with a hacker-like mindset.

There is a huge opportunity for connected car product developers to build intrusion detection devices to block hackers and give control back to car consumers. This is a whole industry waiting to be built out, similar to virus and child protection software available for computers.

Maybe you will build secure systems for the connected car ecosystem in cars, dealer software systems and all devices that connect to cars.

8.3 Flying Drones

We have heard about Amazon planning drones for product delivery to our doors. Drone delivery transportation is becoming a reality. Matternet ONE offers the first smart weather resistant drone for autonomous transportation in locations without roads to carry payloads up to 20km in a single charge. Facebook is using its own Drones to provide wireless access to rural South Africa. Drones were used in getting pictures of the 2015 Nepal earthquakes for remote workers. They are being tested as first-responder vehicles for a fire and saving endangered animals in the Himalayas.

Figure 19 Matternet ONE Transportation Drone

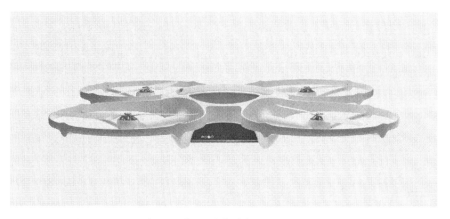

Image Copyright Matternet

As a business, Drones or Unmanned Aerial Vehicles (UAV) as they are called have to get security and privacy compliance and Government approvals to fly in the skies. The products have been iterated well on flight controllers, autopilot features and on board accelerators to stabilize the ride. They can still be improved to bring their costs down. As new industries such as Agriculture, Mapping and Aerial Transportation evolves, there will be a need to iterate and optimize the products for new customer use cases.

8.4 Car Augmenting the Human Experience

Artificial Intelligence is being applied to develop products that augment the human experience inside a car.

Road fatigue with long distance driving is a huge problem that leads to accidents. IBM has developed a telematics device called Artificial Passenger that engages a driver with verbal interactions, looks for driver falling asleep patterns and advises the driver to take a break.

Building the technology is one side of the problem. Getting legal compliance and consumer acceptance are huge problems that will take time in building connected car augmenting solutions.

As affective computing, the science of building machines to develop empathy evolves, you could build cars that can understand the mood of the driver and react to their road rage or somber moods by adjusting the Internet connected entertainment system or warning other drivers on the road to watch out for its angry driver.

As with futuristic technologies, such products will have to bear the risk of creating a new market and the ones with the right customer experience will engage the customer and become the market leader.

CHAPTER 9: Smart Cities

Cities exist because of the fundamental need for humans to connect to each other. Cities bring a variety of people from different towns or other remote places to gel into a more diverse group. People come to cities because of the economic opportunities but share connections to find solutions to common problems across multiple demographics of race, age, interests, concerns etc. slicing us into multiple groups creating common threads of bonds from common problems and opportunities.

Hence Smart cities come with many different definitions and expectations from different stakeholders. Businesses, government, consumers, non-profits, schools, etc. all compete and collaborate to create the vibrancy of each city. People who want to preserve the history and those who want whole new transformation, people who want technology to solve their daily problems such a traffic and people who want technology to be invisible and create a new fabric of life that's more convenient all make up a city. They push and pull at the priority of what makes their city smart.

This offers a unique opportunity for entrepreneurs to build connected city products focusing on areas that they are passionate to solve for their cities.

Smart cities are evolving with many different applications to reduce costs and improve efficiencies adjusting for each city's need.

9.1 Smart Grids

Solar panels on our rooftops, electric vehicle charger such as Blink are all smart devices sending information on our consumption patterns for service efficiency. Pacific Gas and Electric PG&E in US has switched to smart meters that send them hourly meter readings. Now that we can see our energy usage patterns, the electric company can get automatic outage detection. This allows companies to provide better service and charge us with a metered rating per hour tailored to our usage.

9.2 Connected Parking

Barcelona has become a connected city with smart parking meters and smart bus stops operating on citywide Wi-Fi. The smart IoT devices provide constant data to help residents find parking spots, and get information about commuter options. It helps the city officials with urban planning and crime prevention by looking at the data trends to spot pockets in the city that need their attention.

9.3 Waste Management

Large waste bins in Barcelona have sensors that notify the city for pickup on demand. Compostology is a US based startup that provides smart waste management solution with a device that takes a picture of the inside of a Garbage Bin to check if it is full.

Figure 20 Smart Garbage Waste Bin in Barcelona

9.4 Intelligent Traffic Control

Traffic sensors have adorned city streets for decades and faced the challenge to providing reliable data to help solve the traffic problems. With IoT there is a rebirth of the traffic sensors with intelligent Internet connected sensors and predictive analysis done on the vast volume of data. This is done in several cities around the world in partnership with universities.

Transpose India is a connected city project from CEPT University, Ahmedabad India. It has developed intelligent sensors to monitor data to understand traffic patterns and consumer driving patterns to solve for traffic congestion.

9.5 Smart Lighting

Cities are upgrading their lights to become smart connected lights that offer energy efficient LED lights with sensors tracking crowds of people around it and connecting on a mesh network. Glasgow has setup smart lights in three locations. The lights can notify the city when bulbs need replacement, monitor their environment for disturbances and can be remotely increased for brightness by 30% in case of an emergency. They also have added sensors to collect Urban Informatics such as air quality, sound levels and offer limited Wi-Fi access around it.

The city of Los Angeles has implemented Philips CityTouch connected light management system allowing for the city to manage each light including legacy lights and those of other manufacturers using a remote mobile app and cloud service.

Connected city is also a growing job market for students to innovate to build smart cities.

9.6 Urban Informatics

Urban Informatics refers to the data a city collects to create transparency and solve problems for its citizens. This includes data from sensors for traffic monitoring, smart lighting, city parking usage patterns, air quality data, noise levels and pedestrian traffic levels.

Figure 21 London City Dashboard

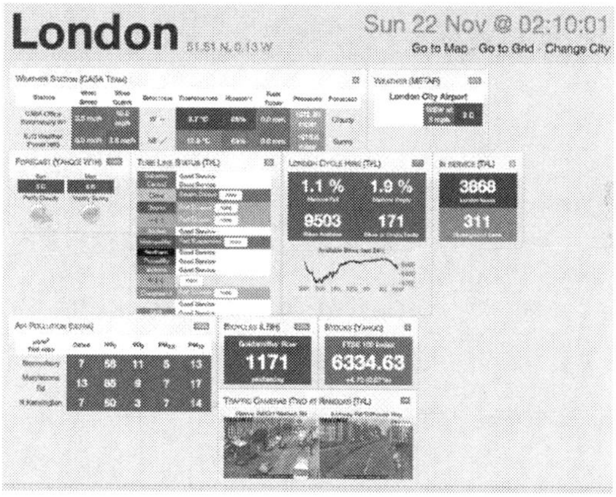

Image Copyright Sudha Jamthe

Air Quality Monitoring

Air Quality is a very important aspect of the quality of any city resident's life. There are experiments by people done to measure a city's air quality by attaching sensors on bicycle.

Opensensors.io has done a community project by bringing many stakeholders around Heathrow airport neighborhood to put air sensors to measure pollution levels and factors that could be causing pollution from airport traffic. Atmotube has piloted a personal Air quality monitor breaking challenges of measuring the accuracy of the pollutants consistently.

The power of an IoT Product comes from real time monitoring driving actions. A huge challenge with real time Air Quality measurement comes from the existing practice of measuring pollution changes in pollution over a month or a year with no agreed metric across cities or different stakeholders on a metric for real time air quality measurement. This makes it a challenge to present data insights to stakeholders causing pollution who maybe denying the scale of their impact.

9.7 Unique Flavor of Smart Cities

9.7.1 City Solving for Domestic violence

The cities of the world are becoming smart by changing to Smart Lights, Smart Traffic Controls and then adding on other Connected Smart Services. Each city of the world has its own problems, culture and its own priorities. That influences how the city becomes a smart city. Miguel Rodrigues, CEO and General Manager of Smartcities2020 platform has been implementing smart city solutions for Sao Paolo where he builds smart city solutions for entertainment in Malls. Miguel Rodrigues says, "*Look at Jamaica. They do not want Internet access at the city center; instead they want to use the connectedness of their cities to focus on women equality and stop domestic violence*"

Dazl.io has created an IoT Product to help women in India protect themselves from rape. This is the beginning of each city adopting IoT to solve their unique problems.

9.7.2 Beacons For Social Good

City of Amsterdam has created the World's First Internet of Things lab called **iBeacon Living Lab** (http://ibeaconlivinglab.com/) and the Beacon Mile.

This is a set of sensors along a public path including a library, a canal, a bicycle bridge and museum. They have made it open source for the public to access these beacons to test out use cases for a connected city that goes beyond large businesses to social good apps.

Figure 22 Amsterdam Beacon Mile with Jonathan Carter of Glimworm

Image Copyright Sudha Jamthe

This has further inspired entrepreneurs to create "The Things Network" http://thethingsnetwork.org/ a public network of LoRA WAN gateways to create a crowd sourced open source IoT connectivity for the whole city of Amsterdam. This is a classic example of an IoT Disruption that started with a city and a citizen now creating a new innovation movement to improve IoT connectivity globally.

9.8 Challenges in building out Smart cities

The challenges of building a connected or smart city lie in change management in a city among multiple stakeholders, lack of clarity of who owns the new infrastructure costs and need to bring citizens to participate and utilize the new smart products to generate scale of adoption while maintaining the very fabric that makes the city.

The challenges do not lie in the technical ability of the city to measure city data but it measuring it correctly and in presenting the data using a common language among stakeholders who are not used to work together.

For e.g. opensensors.io created a community of sensors around Heathrow airport to measure air quality. They realized the need to place sensors everywhere and not where they are likely to provide more data because that will bias the data set. Also presenting the data in a way all stakeholders can define the problem in the same way is important to start discussions for change among people not used to working together.

CHAPTER 10: IIoT Business Model Evolutions

Bosch Group in Germany has established an Internet of Things and Services Lab in partnership with the University of St Gallen in Switzerland to explore and test the potential for IoT to create new business models.

Industrial IoT has many evolving business models. Karsten Königstein CEO of Smartly Solutions from Germany who worked with Bosch says, "IoT can offer many value with measurable ROI. It offers two way digital communications inside the factory floor replacing paper. It helps logistics track stock in the production floor and also during transportation. More business models will evolve in industries as we test and iterate new innovation with Internet of Things."

Mini-Case study 16:

IoT Innovation: Wearable for the Factory

Business: ProGlove

Value from the Connected Device: ProGlove offers a glove for the manufacturing assembly line worker. It has an attachable RFID reader that scans items in the manufacturing process and sends the data to the cloud improving quality and speed of manufacturing steps. It improves speed because the worker does not have to pick a RFID reader to get the reading separate from the assembly process. It also improves the quality of the assembly line by tracking for any missing steps in the assembly process from the data gathered.

Business Case:

ProGlove helps manufacturing automobile customers create efficiency from speed, quality and improved operations.

ProGlove has made strategic business decisions that have helped them scale. They focus on car manufacturing instead of making it a broader manufacturing play. This has helped them understand the assembly line process, where there can be improvements.

They have added RFID as a detachable attachment to their glove to offer backward compatibility to RFID scanner processing. They can adapt to new improvements by adding more attachments in the future.

ProGlove has created a new market category for itself and is growing with focus.

Part III: Disruptive Innovations of Industries

"*Smart mobile health platforms can act as integrators connecting data gathered from IoT devices and health data such as blood tests, medical history and genetics, environmental, social economics data. They can then analyze these data and its impact on causation, treatment and outcome of diseases and provide personalized recommendations to patients*" - **Tatyana Kanzaveli Founder and CEO, Open Health Network.**

CHAPTER 11: Connected Devices in Retail

"Today's students are digital natives. We have integrated mobile technology into our lives. With the inception of the Internet of Things, digital native graduates are at the intersection of a new industry that will make us question why everything is not connected to our devices." - Paul Heayn, MBA graduate and mobile product manager

It is a retailer's dream to know their customer behavior as they navigate through the purchase funnel from traffic to consideration to purchase. IoT devices collect massive volume of data about customers. The key in understanding opportunities in Retail and IoT is connectivity. IoT offer three types of connectivity, each with its own set of opportunities.

11.1   Contextual   Connectivity   for Personalization

IoT provides data along with context of the customer. **It tells us the location of the customer, their moods and how focused the customer** is. For example a Fitbit does not only show the numbers of steps taken and calories burnt but consistency of such behavior indicates that the customer is a much more deliberate focused person. A customer who is able to focus their health habits to consistency is likely to show a focused behavior on their research to purchase a product than do binge shopping or buy random things. This impacts the experience that should be provided in the purchase flow for the customer instead of dependency on merchandising for cross-sells.

Mini-Case study 17:

IoT Innovation: Facial Recognition in Retail Store

Business: Altromercato Italian retailer

Value from the Connected Device:

Facial recognition shared from retail stores gives information about customer demographics to retailer.

Business Value:

Altromercato is an Italian retailer with 300 chain stores. They have embarked on a pilot to add sensors that combine beacons, a camera and Wi-Fi to it stores in Milan and Genoa. They use facial recognition on customers visiting different store locations and find demographics of customers. They quickly adapt each store location merchandising strategy to meet the customer They also test for the effectiveness of their front display and how long customers stay in the store.

This helps the store stock and display the right merchandise that will be likely to be purchased by the customer and increases their revenues while making the customers happy.

Intel is working with Octoblu on a similar retail pilot in US. Octoblu is a plug and play IoT Platform with an easy visual interface to connect heterogeneous sensors and devices to each other. This pilot includes retail use cases to use facial recognition to understand customer demographics similar to Altromercato's pilot in Italy.

The real business opportunity is waiting for innovation from product and business managers on how to productize this experience to create value to engage and earn the trust of the customer. Intel-Octoblu pilot is testing customer purchase behavior by customizing store music, offering personalized mobile offers and Display Ads to the customer.

Customers will be privacy conscious about the data collected about their shopping behavior. So the Product Manager has the challenge to communicate what the retailer has collected and get their permission to use it to present use cases that enable more shopping.

11.2 Analytics of Paper

Newspapers and Magazines are a shrinking market but they sell ads to drive brand awareness and conversion for products in an increasingly digitized world.

Imagine Analytics from paper! What if paper was a connected product and you could click it at different places and it leads to different digitized experiences and you can track the analytics of the clicks to understand user behavior similar to an eCommerce site. Razorfish Germany did just that and executed it brilliantly as an Audi Brochure that comes to life when you place a mobile phone on a page.

Razorfish Germany team built a connected paper IoT product using Novartis's Dr.Kate Stone's electronic printed ink (add to index different from electronic ink).

IoT Technology behind the Audi TT Brochure

Razorfish team has solved the interactive design challenge by bringing the Audi TT brochure to life. They have used a Nodex Bluetooth chip hidden between the pages to provide the sensor and connectivity of the brochure to a mobile app. Each tap triggers a different experience on the mobile app and brings the brochure to life.

Analytics of Paper

Typically for a digital ad we can get impressions, clicks, conversions and demographics of the user. Imagine a separate code behind the Audi TT brochure can track brochures given to men or women, tracking their behavioral differences signally their difference in features of the car. EU has tight data sharing policies so data can be gathered only to improve overall user experience nothing else.

11.3 Zero Click Commerce

Internet of Things offers multiple customer touch points while the customer deliberates a purchase. IoT devices provide data while the customer jogs, sleeps, eats and walks. **A connected customer is an engaged customer because each touch point gives data insights about the customer's behavior.** This will help the retailer understand the customer better and reduce friction in the commerce experience and personalize the customer's optimal experience flow to purchase and retention.

IoT has taken the Commerce experience from 1-click to 0-click commerce. The Amazon Dash Button is a classic example of that. It allows customers to tap a button pre-programmed to order commodity items around the house. Your coffee maker orders coffee, washer orders soap, fridge orders eggs, medicine cabinets order medicine prescription and pet dispenser re-orders pet food. **This is what I call as 0-click commerce, total frictionless commerce.** This is action by the customer pre-decided to trust Amazon to order refills once the item reaches a certain inventory level made possible only by the proliferation of smart devices connected to the Internet.

Amazon owns 1-click shopping on the web. So it is not a surprise for Amazon to make our long-due dream of making our household appliances smart - with 1-click push of a button with the Amazon Dash Button

Mini-Case study 18:

IoT Innovation: Amazon Dash 1-click IoT Button

Business: Amazon

Product Innovation: The button is designed with the tap of the button synonymous to the 1-click action we associate with Amazon brand and how it reduces friction in purchasing non-fun essential items like soap, coffee, garbage bags, printer paper, shaving cream and diapers. And it seamlessly extends Amazon's commerce business right into our home.

The Product Design of The Amazon Dash Button

It appears that the button is a Bluetooth device that communicates with Amazon App on your smartphone and uses the Phone's connection to order online. Amazon is giving a custom button for each brand so it simplifies it for consumers to order particular consumables. So you get a button for Tide and stick it to your washing machine and another button for your coffee maker. Each Bluetooth device has a unique Mac address. When you set it up first time, it will tie to your Amazon identity and let you configure some sizes/quantity/type of the item to get to a particular SKU in Amazon's catalog. Subsequently when you press the button it tells the App to order that item and sends an alert giving the user the freedom to cancel the order.

Once you order the item, subsequently the order tracking comes via mobile alerts using Amazon app.

IoT Design Simplicity extended to Commerce Experience

The beauty of IOT devices compared to all tech innovations of the past is how we are seeing simplicity in design and the good ones tie seamlessly to a mobile App.

Amazon Dash Button is a simple button you can stick anywhere on any appliance to remind you to order the refills. It ties to the Amazon App and allows you to cancel your order giving user the choice to do comparison-shopping. This is such a subtle feature that builds trust with users challenging them that Amazon has the best price. It builds on Amazon's delivery convenience. It offers features to track the purchase which all ties back to existing Amazon App.

The Data Behind the Dash Button

I wonder what Amazon data says about the buying habit of people who buy consumables online. Do we go to Amazon to buy Diapers and end up purchasing lots of other stuff promoted to us? Now will there be any cannibalization of such spending from users?

It is possible that some product manager inside Amazon looked at this data and said, this is still the right thing for the customer so let's do it and went ahead. Maybe they estimated the upside from the scale of new purchases from the Dash button and the increased trust from Prime customers offsetting this loss (if any).

Value from the Connected Device:

With the Dash Button Amazon offers the IOT device, the App, the platform and owns the inventory of the brand consumables. So they are able to offer a seamless frictionless experience for the consumer setting it up for success.

Business Value:

Amazon owns the distribution of Prime customers where they have solved for the delivery problem. Any other retailer will have the problem of on-boarding users to adopt a new technology. This connects seamlessly to Amazon's inventory (for most cases). So they are deployed it for Prime customers only at launch, thereby strengthening the value of Amazon Prime memberships.

The only challenge with this product is that we have to setup a button for each brand item.

I see Amazon's DRS (Dash Replenishment Service) replace the individual buttons and get them baked into various equipments by the manufacturer offering the buttons as part of their device to offer consumable replenishment from Amazon.

11.4 Retail Stores and Chat Commerce

Let us look at what opportunity does a connected customer offer for retail by wearing a smart wearable device and making their behavioral data available to retailers.

Join me in imagining the story of the data from wearable devices differently. The fitness tracker will tell you more about your moods than just track how much you walked today. Health and sleep monitor tells you more about behavior and intent than just health.

If you combine data from the fitness tracker and sleep monitor, you can find out if the health conscious customer is doing a deliberate list based shopping with focus or is the customer doing binge shopping because he is stressed and sleep deprived. Such data will be a boon to retailers to merchandise the right products to increase their sales.

11.4.1. Geofencing and iBeacons

Retailers implement beacons in stores and connect to their own mobile apps.

Retailers can know when a customer is in their store by using

Geofencing on IoT devices. The company estimote offers a beacon that restaurants can place in tables and allows customer to pay from their seats using a mobile app. Coupa Café in Palo Alto, California is an example of a restaurant who uses Estimote for geofencing making the food ordering and payment frictionless in ways not possible without smart connected devices.

In 2015 Target, Home Depot and Macy's, all large Retailers in America have set up Bluetooth sensors called "Beacons" from Estimote or Shopkick in select stores to connect to customer apps to create customized experiences based on geofencing customers. They have the ability to collect data about customer behavior in their stores to learn about customer's shopping habits inside their stores.

A startup called Sense360 offers behavioral data about customers from a combination of sensors inside their iPhones to create invisible apps that connect to other mobile apps at gas stations, stores and libraries.

KLM Airlines deployed beacons to provide airport navigation for passengers in transit to another terminal by using its own app. JFK airport in New York deployed a system called The BlipTrack system using beacons at TSA checkpoints that uses passenger's mobile phones to measure how long people are taking to go through the lines. Both have different technology implementations and challenges of deployment to scale. It is important to use these sensors with the permission of users; else it will break customer trust and disrupt businesses negatively.

I haven't seen my favorite use case in any store yet! Imagine if retail store kiosks can interact with a wearable device as the user enters the store and allows the user to order in a single click without the long process of going around the store and deliberating on purchases or to order shipping of items when the inventory is available in another store.

11.4.2 Chat Commerce with Beacons

Sensora, a sensor manufacturer from China has created an integration with WeChat, the largest chat app in China with 650 Million monthly active users. Sensora has deployed Beacons in retail stores and tracks users using WeChat App. This has created a whole new dimension of commerce inside the chat app and created a new Ad model tied to the sensors in the stores.

Mini-Case study 19:

IoT Innovation: Beacons in Retail tied to Chat App

Business: Sensora and WeChat

Value from Connected Device: Beacons identify location of users at different retail stores making it easy for Sensora and the

---

retailer to target the user.

Product Innovation: Sensora has connected their Beacon Platform with WeChat chat app in China saving retailers trouble of distributing their apps to talk to their beacons.

Business Value:

Sensora a large sensor marker from China has partnered with WeChat and integrated their beacon geofencing platform. Then they have begun deploying Beacons in thousands of stores including Pizza Hut in China. When a customer enters a PizzaHut store their WeChat app talks to the beacons and knows the location of the user. Then Sensora via WeChat sends coupons to the users to use in store and also socially share to other customer.

They use this data to learn what items in the menu is liked and widely shared by customers to help the retailer adapt their menu selection.

Sensora has successfully scaled geo-fencing access to customers for retailers by partnering with WeChat and offering an integrated customer experience.

The tight integration between Sensora and WeChat and clear

ownership of Sensora owning the retail customers is a good example of a partnership and multi-company IoT customer experience. However the data being collected by Sensora via WeChat App may not be permitted legally everywhere in the world. In Europe the customer will have to be notified about data collected about them and how this data is being shared. So the product design will have to get the user's permission for their data.

Many Smart LED Lights come with Bluetooth beacons make it easy for retailers and also warehouses to replace their lights and get connected stores as a bonus to go with it.

The market for connected lights is growing with Bluetooth connected lights from GE, Misfit Bolt and ilumi. Bytelight has taken a different approach to connected lights and provides the software infrastructure to connect any light to become a connected light in a Retail indoor setting.

Visible Light Communication (VLC), is the connected light standard setup by Philips and supported by many in this space.

Retailers can learn customer behavior of preferred shopping isles, areas of engagement and real-time monitoring of customers in-store with connected lights. However privacy of the user is an open issue that needs to be solved before retailers can scale this opportunity. Hence usage of connected LED lights in retail is in early stages with opportunity ripe for innovation.

Can you create apps that add value to customers from the data from connected retail lights? Then you can get the customer's permission to collect their data making it a win-win for the customer and retailer.

CHAPTER 12: Connected Device in Healthcare

Health was the first industry where Internet of Things touched consumers directly and is the top industry disrupted because it has woken up consumers about the power of their health data.

Internet of Things came to Healthcare in the form of wearable Fitness Trackers. Now we are seeing non-fitness personal products and a new type of wearables that are inside our bodies. This has created the new area of Digital Health.

12.1 Wearables and Health Informatics

Wearables like Fitbit started tracking the fitness health of users with social features to share their data to friends. It has expanded to track health vitals such as pulse, blood pressure etc. beyond exercising to daily health monitoring. Health tracking started with the early adopters of exercise conscious adults and has expanded to health monitoring for seniors, babies and pets. Today it includes sleep monitoring and provides data about sleep cycles leading to questions about stress and lifestyle of the individual impacting their health.

Apple offers the Apple Watch as a wearable device, Healthkit for developers and Health App for users of iOS devices.

Figure 23 Apple's Health App

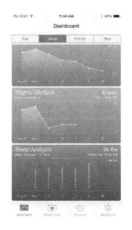

Image Copyright Sudha Jamthe

Apple Watch measures all the ways a user moves. It differentiates between walking the dog, climbing stairs, or playing with kids. Health kit allows iOS apps from developers that collect health and fitness information to store user data securely in a central location and gives control to users on what app can share what data with Apple's Health App. For example I use Steps+ App to track how I meet my 10,000 steps goals each day and SleepTime App to monitor my sleeping pattern and see a combined dashboard in the Health App on my iPhone.

All wearables are not fitness bands. Imec offers an EKG necklace and Preventive checks for cardiac monitoring, arrhythmia detection, stress monitoring, and epilepsy monitoring. Neumitra's biowatch measures the sympathetic nervous system to track stress.

Power of Health Informatics

The real power of Health tracking wearables in the data they provide. Storage and processing of health data is called Health Informatics.

Consumers using various wearable fitness trackers are becoming more health conscious as they are seeing their own fitness data daily and are comparing them with friends in social networks.

Access to our own health data is empowering us to have a dialog with their doctors to make informed healthcare choices. Recently, I saw my pulse shoot up when I checked my blood pressure at home. When I visited the doctor my pulse levels were normal. I started wearing a Basis Peak wearable watch and could track the trend of my pulse and went back to my doctor to have an informed discussion and ask questions about my health care options.

Microsoft HealthVault and Google Health have failed with similar offerings in the past.

Apple HealthKit connects to Mayo clinic and Epic systems the electronic health records vendor. This allows for healthcare providers to intervene with patients who show out of normal range health data.

I have not seen Hospitals or healthcare providers offer consumer services based data from Healthkit or any Wearable Health data integration. Yet.

Challenges and Opportunity for Health Tech Entrepreneurs

This is an opportunity ripe for entrepreneurs and product managers of healthcare technology companies because consumers want this integration.

Healthcare industry comes with strict compliance requirements to handle consumer health data to protect the privacy and security of consumers' healthcare data. US has Health Insurance Portability & Accountability Act (HIPAA) while European Union has EU's Directive on Data Protection and Canada has Canada's Personal Information Protection and Electronic Documents Act

(PIPEDA) for any organization handling, storing and transferring patient information. This is a requirement for anyone handling consumer data from wearables and other health devices.

Another challenge that is not yet solved for is clarity on how health insurance companies will use this data once it becomes readily available. Will insurance companies look at consumers who are not exercising enough and charge them higher premium for health insurance coverage?

12.2 Non-wearable Personal Health Products

Many personal products are becoming personal health products by adding sensors and solving for unique problems.

Oral B, Braun and Kolibree have launched smart toothbrushes that track how long and how well did kids brush their teeth and share data with parents. Kolibree presents this data as a fun gaming app for kids thereby making it fun for kids to brush their teeth.

Weighing scales are now connected and help us keep track of our weight trends. Water glass measures the hydration level of people with a cup.

Some of these personal health products offer more health data that empowers consumers further to take charge of their lives.

A new class of products are innovating in whole new areas unrelated to health data. People with Parkinson disease and other neurological disorders have tremors that disrupt their daily activities. Google's Liftware spoon helps them eat independently by reducing tremors by 70% while Arc is a new IoT Product that helps them write with reduced tremors.

These are products that are pure innovations focused on solving a problem for a customer using Internet of Things.

12.3 Digital Health

A new class of Digital Health products are evolving as wearables not on us but inside us.

12.3.1 Cyber implants

Boston University is testing a bionic pancreas with an implantable needle that talks to a Phone and tracks blood sugar levels. Proteus Health offers a FDA approved pill with Ingestion Event Markers to track user's biometrics from inside their bodies. Digital tattoos from Motorola and Vivalink has a NFC based skin tag to unlock your phone securely. University of Illinois has created a skin implant that is a mesh of computer fibers thinner than a human hair that can monitor our body's inner workings from the surface. The Gates Foundation is supporting a MIT project to create an implantable female contraceptive.

12.3.2 Wearables that extend the Brain to IoT

A Brown University project now owned by Braingate, co has created a brain implant called Braingate. When this sensor is implanted into the brain it monitors brain activity and converts the thoughts or neural signals into computer commands.

The sensor consists of 100 thin electrodes and an external prosthetic decoder device. This is in clinical trials to help patients with ALS or Spinal cord injury. Think of the products you can build with this to help disabled people to operate wheelchairs or move other things around them by their thoughts.

12.3.3 Digital Health Product Design

Most health implants talk to a mobile. So for the female contraceptive, a click on a mobile makes a tiny chip inside the woman's body secrete small amounts of contraceptive hormones. Some implants such as the Protheus chat directly with the doctor.

Some of these are futuristic today and will need to iterate to adapt to what is acceptable customer experience for consumers. It is important in all Digital Health products to design the customer experience with sensitivity to the user's adoption and respect for their privacy.

Also technology typically becomes obsolete soon as new models evolve. So great care has to be taken to decide on hardware and software and protocol choices in building implants.

Also health implants have to go through clinical trials before FDA approvals and have to be designed with care to stay relevant for a very long time.

12.3.4 Digital Informatics Insights

There is so much data from wearables, from smart weighing scales, smart toothbrushes, wireless glucose monitors etc.

There are two open opportunities untapped in healthcare space.

First all fitness devices provide raw data trends and stop short of providing actionable insights. What will help the user is to understand the insights behind the data to offer actionable insights. For example Sleep monitors show how many times a user was awake during the night. So its interesting data to know you were stressed and tossing and turning at night. If the health device can provide insight behind the data and tell the user when to get help from their physician, and provide details on their sleep patterns and the impact stress will have on their overall health it will drive actions that was not possible with the IoT.

Secondly the data collected from IoT is about the user's action or what can be gathered live from sensors. This data is today presented in isolation from the user's healthcare data that tells about their health vitals, health history and any conditions they are getting treatment from their medical practitioners. **Integration of these two data will provide useful insights that**

can help the user much more holistically and drive actions that were not possible with the IoT device. This integration has to be done at the cloud by health platforms or health cloud providers. It comes with huge opportunities but also huge challenges of managing the privacy of the user and compliance about protecting their right to who can access their health information.

With wearable market highly fragmented there are many different wearable fitness bands that send data to many different cloud storage platforms. This adds to the complexity of integrating the wearables data to legacy healthcare systems.

12.3.5 Implanted Digital Identity or Verified Self

Swarms of nano-devices called "motes" can organize themselves inside the human body to attack cancer cells or store our information inside us encrypted to store our secure identity. Implanting RFID chips to track a person has uses in tracking military soldiers or a lost child but has serious implications for the privacy of the individual and societal impact of avoiding an Orwelian society.

12.4 IoT in Hospitals and Telemedicine

Hospitals have not yet adopted Health Informatics integrations. Meanwhile there are new innovations coming up in hospitals with new IoT products using Beacons for inside locations tracking of patients to understand their behavior to provide better care using this data.

12.4.1 Children's Health with HAND

HAND is one of the finalists of Barcelona World Smart City Award that has built a health IoT product for children in Hospitals. It offers an innovative platform with multiple Apps for children interactions, immersive experiences, entertainment, fun and education, developed on top of massive sensor and actuators network at hospital environment, improving behaviors monitoring and managing data by the hospital staff.

Birmingham Children's Hospital NHS Foundation Trust (BCH) has piloted HAND with 43,000 inpatients admissions to use the sensors and gaming app environment of HAND platform to learn about hospitalized children's health to inform caregivers to provide optimal care.

12.4.2 TeleMedicine

Telemedicine is the application of technology to provide clinical health care at a distance.

This is an arm of healthcare industry that has been innovating over years focusing on transmission of images and health informatics data across remote systems. Internet of Things helps expedite this innovation adoption with wireless access to patient health in real-time.

Telesurgery trans-Atlantic have been performed by a remote surgeon using robotic arms and high-speed internet connections.

Internet of Things with its power to focus on a simple customer problem found its use with parents of kids who call in sick from school. Parents are troubled to rush to the school to take their child for a doctor's visit only to be asked to wait for some test results and give some pain medication most of the times. It causes loss of productivity and stress in the parents and kids are taken off school only to return back next day saying it was not critical enough to stay off school.

From Sep 2015 Texas in US allow school-based telemedicine visits for children covered by Medicaid. A remote doctor uses an electronic stethoscope to hear the heartbeat and a digital orthoscope to look into a child's ears while the school nurse monitors using a video chat will monitor the child. The doctor then prescribes medicine for pickup from the local pharmacy.

The schools and parents have gone through piloting this earlier and solved for issues around parent consent of children's health data access.

Healthcare space is advancing working with rest of the stakeholders involved to resolve issues with adoption of IoT products. If you are an IoT product maker it is important to note that if you built a digital orthoscope or electronic stethoscope it is not about selling it to doctors to use it though they are the ultimate users of the devices and will need to be trained to use it correctly. It is important to understand whose problem you are solving and develop the right channel to your customers.

When you look at a remote EKG product, think about how it should not be sold to consumers but find its use in telemedicine.

PART IV: VALUE CREATION WITH TECHNOLOGY AND DATA

"The meek shall inherit the earth .. but not it's mineral rights" is a statement attributed to J Paul Getty. I believe IoT, Data and Analytics have the same relationship. There is a lot of Data generated from IoT devices (the Earth) .. but the money (value) is in the analytics (the algorithms)"- **Ajit Jaokar Author "IoT and Data Science" and Instructor Oxford University**

CHAPTER 13: IoT Technology Infrastructure

A typical IoT infrastructure includes the following components.

13.1. To the Edge

The Edge

IoT covers integration of many layers of technologies. IoT device can be a sensor or actuator.

Sensors track changes in temperature, humidity, proximity, light, sound etc. and send a state change to the next layer of the IoT system. E.g. when we leave the garage door open the sensor just sends the information to a local hub or to the cloud.

Actuators take action based on a state change. E.g. a garden hydration system can monitor humidity levels of the soil and turn on the sprinkler.

Hardware Platform Layer

The hardware platform layer goes from the network edge or endpoint of a device to the cloud. This platform includes: 1) the chip layer with security and embedded devices environment 2) Communication layer to send IoT data to various clouds and gateways and 3) Intelligent analytics platform which offers hardware specific analytics associated with motors for preventive maintenance.

Intel offers this as a platform from a chip level. Cisco offers Embedded Service Routers and IOx Application Platform. Samsung offers Artik, an Arduino certified series of kits that connects to SAMI, their Data Driven Development platform with simple open APIs to build and deploy IoT Solutions. There are also several DIY hardware platforms available in open source that we'll learn about shortly.

Gateway or Hub

The data from IoT devices could be processed on site on a hub to take quick action or maybe sent to a cloud for processing. E.g. a home security alarm system typically has an onsite hub that listens to the sensors on different doors and rings the alarm based on the settings on the hub. It also sends data to the cloud to offer remote notification to the users. Gateways are planned for factory environments where it makes sense to process large volume of data onsite to take quick actions.

Communication Layer

IoT devices send their data to Cloud Servers. There are many standards in this layer today – Carrier networks, Wi-Fi-, Bluetooth, ZigBee are a top few.

13.2. Cloud and Fog Computing

Existing cloud infrastructures such as **Amazon Web Services (AWS)** are being leveraged and new IoT cloud platforms are being built out in commercial and open source software.

The cloud acts as the software that connects the IoT device to the Internet. It also communicates between the IoT devices and the users who receive the benefit from the device. At a minimum the cloud platforms have a listener to receive the data from large volume of IoT devices, authenticate the specific devices, store and process large volume of data and send notifications or instructions for actions to receivers which can be the devices or mobile apps.

Many vertical cloud solutions are evolving for specific vertical solutions such as healthcare, automotive etc.

13.3. Mobile Apps

Mobile Apps offer the customer interface for many IoT Product hardware. They also act as the user interface to send notifications to the user using the cloud as an intermediary. For example Alarm.com security app sends notifications and offers its mobile app as the software interface to the user.

Sometimes Mobile Devices also act as IoT devices using their sensors for motion, gyroscope, GPS etc. For example Fitness tracking app Step+ uses motion sensor on iPhone.

CHAPTER 14: The Goldmine of Big Data Analytics

This chapter focuses on Big Data in an IoT Product Development context and offers guidance on where to focus to build product experiences and expose data right to create value for customers to create a successful IoT Business.

Big Data and Data Science in IoT is a vast developing topic. Please refer to 'Data Science and IoT' book by Ajit Jaokar for stats and in-depth reading of this topic.

14.1 Big Data and Sensor Fusion

Big Data Analytics is the backbone of the promise of Internet of Things. IoT devices collect data as a time series and create massive volume of data and create trends. All IoT devices have sensors that track for some changes and collect data points with each change. They watch for certain data triggers to send alerts. For example, a pre-set temperature indicates that the cooking range is left on and sends alert to users to stop a fire.

The volume of data from anticipated 50Bil IoT devices by 2020 creates a big data storage and analytics problem. IoT presents a classic Big data problem because it collects large volume of data, and large types of data from variety of sensors and different formats from variety of IoT products. The data from IoT sensors come in real-time. Sensor Fusion is the term used to refer to combining data gathered from a variety of sensors to develop recommendations.

A startup called Sense360 offers behavioral data about customers from a combination of sensors inside their iPhones to create invisible apps that connect to other mobile apps at gas stations, stores and libraries. For example, they can find out when a customer is inside a gas station before they start paying for gasoline so they can recommend what credit card to use to help a financial client. They do this using a combination of sensors present inside the iPhone.

Data is the real power of IoT as sensors share data that can be turned into insights to drive actions. Some of this data comes with a high throughput; some with high bandwidth and some are spurts of alerts that signal a potential hazard.

This is where analytics comes in to draw insights that is contextual, actionable and offers learning to adjust future behaviors.

14.2 The Power of Predictive Analytics

Health trackers can go from providing trends to actionable insights only when intelligent analysis is done in the context of a person's health data to drive life saving recommendations.

Consumers are beginning to get used to smart devices at home. Nest Thermostat can offer so much convenience to users based on data patterns seen in temperature usage based on when people are away from home and their preferred temperature setting at different times of the day, days of the month etc. all possible from data analysis and personalized home recommendation.

Predictive analytics is successfully used today in manufacturing, airlines and industrial setting to look at data about machines for hazard prevention and proactive estimate of equipment failure patterns. This is saving millions of dollars from avoiding downtime of machines, keeping airlines in the ground from last minute equipment problems.

14.3 Optimizing Product Flow Using Data

Shifting Data from Noise to build IoT Products

There are a variety of IoT Products that use data from a user's movement to create value to users.

For example, Sensoria socks track the running pattern of users to give recommendation for optimal use of their feet during running. Kolibree toothbrush looks at bristles movement from brushing to predict what teeth areas were not brushed properly. Zepp uses player's hand movements to track whether they are playing variety of games with the best swing to make recommendation to improve their game of Tennis, Baseball or Golf. Fitness Sleep monitors track customer's sleep data and derive value from insights from the trends.

All of these solve for a common data problem of filtering noise from data. This is similar to how sound speakers provide noise filtering to help us enjoy music better. They must develop data algorithms to find patterns to separate out noise from actual player movements to create their data set before they develop recommendations.

This is a fun challenge for the product manager to build these algorithms and test them to iterate to develop these products.

Figure 24: Sleep Data From Fitness Band

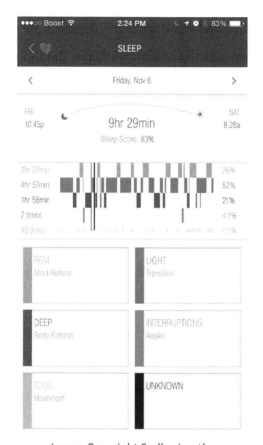

Image Copyright Sudha Jamthe

Brain Inspired Computing Hardware

IBM's SyNAPSE chip is modeled after the human brain. Such a chip can help build devices that can understand context with multiple variables such as who, where, what similar to the brain processing information from multiple sensors.

All this produces data that should be optimized to create product flows to solve for unique problems of the future.

14.4 Virtualization and presentation of data

The application of IoT data spans from supply chain, CRM to city Informatics to Retailers.

The key to successful adoption of insights from this data hinges on the virtualization and presentation of data insights to cater to multiple stakeholders to be inspired enough to accept changes to existing systems and processes.

City Informatics

Cities collect massive volume of data from hundreds of thousands of data points from parking meters, traffic sensors and usage patterns of public commuter options. At its basic level it can provide education to the public. City officials can use the data patterns to understand how to adjust infrastructure spending to help the city's residents optimally. Predictive Analytics will help the city understand the patterns in the data to draw insights on the city's residents usage pattern and predict traffic demand, estimate number of parking spaces needed and even plan hosting large events in the city to manage tourism better.

Retail Data

Retailers can benefit from the integrated data gathered about consumer behavior using wearable devices. Strap is a wearables platform that integrates data from many wearables opted by users willingly and develops insights for retailers to use to offer relevant purchase coupons. For example, a retailer who knows that a customer walks to work daily can offer a walking shoes ad or coupon instead of a generic product offer.

Industrial Data

Data from sensors in agricultural setting when acted upon in real-time can improve massive volume of crop yields. Industrial predictive data about machines and quality control data should be integrated to existing systems to develop meaningful insights.

For all these it is important to present the data in dashboards with the right amount of customization to present to multiple stakeholders.

14.5 Data Science and IoT

Machine learning is the part of computer technique that uses statistical techniques to construct a model from observed data instead of the user pre-defining rules to create the model. It can be simple linear regression. It depends on the quality of data fed that represents the feature set needed to build the model.

Deep learning is a broader type of Machine Learning where the computer will learn and form its own feature set and then apply statistics to construct a model. This can be used to build classifications or predictions.

Machine Learning is used in image, speech recognition and gesture recognition in the world of IoT Products. Deep Learning takes this one step further and improves the accuracy of the predictions.

For example, the spam detector for emails is run using machine learning. Facebook, Apple and Google use machine learning for image recognition.

Deep Learning can offer amazing applications when looking at images or videos from IoT Products.

For example, in a crowded stadium or carnival, a child separated from a parent can be spotted with high confidence by a predictive model using deep learning to recognize faces and looking for the parent and child images that were together and now are separated in the crowd.

My personal favorite is for citizen home cameras to track flooding creeks behind my house to predict for floods in our neighborhoods when water level rises in houses upstream.

There are many untapped innovations waiting to be built with Data Science and IoT.

PART V: THE FUTURE WITH INTERNET OF THINGS

"In Internet of Things 2.0 we are going to add emotions to devices. We have to learn to deal with it when machines have feelings, dreams and memories like in the iRobot movie. Can you image how you will react when your shopping cart says you are pushing it too hard?" **– Ahmed Banafa, College of Engineering, Professor San Jose State University**

CHAPTER 15: IoT Changing the Jobs Landscape

"IoT solutions tend to be complex -- with local sensors, mobile apps, massively scaled cloud infrastructures and long-duration interactions. At the same time, our millions of users need simple user experiences. As today's IoT product managers, we must understand end-to-end systems and also have some design 'taste.' We have to collaborate effectively with mixed teams of developers and interaction designers. And we have to deliver products that are a joy to use – that make the wondrous look easy." – Rich Mironov long-time product management advocate and CEO, Mironov Consulting and Author 'The Art of Product Management'.

15.1 A Student Advantage

Internet of Things is at a pivotal stage where it is picking up scale now in 2015 with a projected growth to 20Bil devices by 2020. Many of us who have seen the Internet boom of late 90s compare IoT today to 1995 period. The innovation in IoT is at an early stage requiring passionate minds that can boldly innovate, iterate and create new solutions not limited to what was possible with the Web. Who better than students graduating now for the next five years fit that profile?

Students are at an advantage, as they do not carry the old knowledge or baggage of what worked or did not work in the Web. Students graduating today have grown up with mobile devices iPhones and Androids and think and use mobile flows intuitively. Internet of Things is natural for them to use to extend mobile devices to connected devices. They can look at connected devices and come up with new user flows, use cases and business models and solutions to problems the world has taken for granted. For example we spent hundreds of years assuming we had to go to the market to buy things. Retailers still thrive on foot traffic to stores. We have created whole shopping cultures with Malls. eCommerce and mCommerce have been incrementally improving offering shopping and fast shipping of items for a fee. Taking the burden off the consumer to track inventory level of consumables and allowing industrial devices to re-order agreed items from trusted retailers is a disruption going beyond shopping using IoT such as Amazon Dash and Flic buttons.

Students entering new jobs can able learn new technologies and think of creative ways to break the barriers of software and hardware interactions creating more efficient IoT infrastructures and communication solutions.

Hungry students are open to take risks and will help create new startups to speed the much-needed iterative cycle of innovation execution to get us to scale IoT technologies to a stable place.

15.2 Job Opportunities

15.2.1 Role of Product Managers

IoT Technologies is in early stages of evolution. The role of the Product manager that is a pivot role in technology is most important and most impacted by IoT. **Product managers are needed to adapt to changes to build the product flows and optimal integration points.** They are needed to **adapt to the change in how IoT changes the product's interaction with customers**. For example customers were used to their oven and fridges do their work quietly. Now with smart devices, the customer is empowered to get notifications alerts and data trends as part of the product experience.

The challenge for Product Managers is also because earlier they were software or hardware product managers except for few embedded devices. **Now the Product managers have to have knowledge of embedded systems, communication layers, Internet cloud technologies and mobile app development for end-to-end IoT device customer flow.** They will have to choose smartly even if they chose to partner with some other company that provides part of the step along the way.

15.2.2 Changing Developer Jobs

The jobs in Cloud and Open source are in two key areas but there are untapped potential in many more areas.

Embedded system developers are in demand to build out the IoT devices. Cloud **Infrastructure developers** are in huge demand to build out the integration points which is different for different industries, to build our sustainable architecture for uptime and scaling of IoT devices connected to their cloud. There are many cloud platform players evolving who are hiring and need to scale cloud developers who understand the complexities involved with embedded systems.

The other jobs are **product managers** whose roles are evolving to understand embedded hardware and cloud infrastructure software for many integration and platform products and newly coming up private cloud solutions. Designers are in demand to design wonderful IoT devices and to create customer flows that are frictionless in an evolving new world.

Open source developers and IoT board (Soc) developers have been innovating already independently and in big companies and have so much work to do to bring about standardization and consolidation of this space in the next three years.

15.2.3 Healthcare

Health trackers market is ripe with many devices. So there are many jobs for product managers, product marketers and data analysts for each of these brands in many global or local brands.

There is much opportunity for **big data analysts** to provide insights from the health data from fitness tracker devices. There is an untapped potential for **developers** to build new apps using Apple WatchKit to solve solutions in healthcare using the health tracking space.

System integrators and health platform provides who understand the privacy and compliance issues with healthcare who can now understand IoT and integrate both data from IoT devices and the patient's healthcare data in a meaningful way have so many startup and job opportunities **to build cloud infrastructure**, **data integration**, data analytics to develop and present insights.

There is a new **demand for design work** to present the data insights to the medical practitioners and consumers. The fitness tracking space is getting so crowded that there is immediate need for excellent **product marketers** to help the evolving brands with their positioning, understanding competitive landscape and communication of their differentiated offering to their customer segments.

There are **sales roles** with creating distribution and sales channels for the devices to consumers. These and some program management roles will switch from existing sales or PMO roles to IoT focused roles.

15.2.4 Analytics and Data Science

Business Intelligence Analysts and Data Scientist are needed to make sense of the data to develop insights that drives actions in real time that were not possible earlier. These have general **data science roles and also industry domain specific business intelligence** and analysis experience for specific industry such as ecommerce, healthcare, marketing insights etc.

The data analysis needs of healthcare are different from that of an industrial IoT and requires domain knowledge for the analyst.

The data analysts are also in huge demand with new products evolving which offer data management platforms for IoT systems.

15.3 Changing Job Landscape

15.3.1 Top IoT Jobs in Demand

One key job in IoT is infrastructure. Since all IoT devices send data and notifications using a cloud, it is very critical to build a scalable cloud solution to keep track of how many concurrent sockets are open, how much data is transacted whether is a public or private cloud solution. **Developers experience in cloud software, cloud architects** who can maintain scalability and uptime are in demand. Several cloud infrastructures coming up for specific verticals require platform developers with specific domain knowledge and knowledge of specific systems for integration such as Sales Force or Health Management Platforms.

15.3.2 Impact of Kickstarter and Indiegogo

Social fundraising platforms Kickstarter and Indiegogo have created a new paradigm for creators of new IoT Technology to get initial funding and market validation from consumers. This has enabled entrepreneurs to create IoT startups globally and build out initial teams and jobs and build out IoT technologies.

They range from full products such as Pebble Watch which raised

$10Million to new ones covering smart lights, tracking devices, home automation hubs, gesture and button devices, DIY kits, smart alarms, music systems, meters, plugs etc.

Wearable Private Cloud revault.io marketed that they will be launching on Indiegogo and built out a mailing list to be notified on launch. This has smartly turned startup outreach and access to talent upside down.

It also a great source for someone seeking employment in IoT startups to comb through the list of startups and reach out to them and find out a way to contribute and drive the innovation in their new jobs.

I do not mind repeating this important job again. **IxD or Interactive Designers are in huge demand**. IoT presents new data and convenience to users from sources such as ARM chips and industrial instruments that are not used to communicating with customers. So interactive designers who can create the clean flow are in demand. Needless to say each IoT device that touches the consumer be in Amazon Dash or a new device such as Vessyl or wearables have set a new standard for amazing minimalistic hardware design and beautiful colors.

Embedded software developers are in demand. Today much of the work is in lower level software with C or C like languages and Linux. As cloud solutions such as AppleWatch and open platforms for IoT cloud evolve the programming can be done in higher-level languages such as **Python, Java and even visual programming** language such a scratch creating demand for programmers. All new systems require **Quality engineers and testers**. IoT coming with many layers of integration will require sophisticated integration testers who can simulate various conditions and understand hardware and software interfaces.

Most IoT devices come with companion apps on Mobile. So **Mobile App developers both iOS and Android are in huge demand** scaling with each new IoT device being launched daily globally.

IoT jobs expand to **car dealers who will have to be tech savvy** to educate consumers on features of the connected cars. Same for **medical** practitioners who will face more informed consumers coming to them with data from their wearable devices.

15.3.3 IoT Job Source

Angel List tracks 350+ startups jobs in INTERNET OF THINGS

CHAPTER 16: IoT Meets Artificial Intelligence

Re-published from my post on TechCrunch from Oct 16 2015

My kitchen opens up to my family room and right smack in the middle sits "Alexa", an Amazon Echo device. It feels strange to call Alexa a device because she has been chatting with my family and is building out her personality. Tell Alexa "You are stupid" and she will reply "I'll try to do better next time" and "That's not very nice to say' the second time. As Amazon applies machine learning Alexa will learn and develop her personality to fit in my home different from yours. Ask her "How are you so smart" and she replies "I was made by a group of very smart people and I am constantly improving my mind". A device with a mind! It reminds me of "Suny" from the movie iRobot. How far fetched is it to think that Alexa will one day differentiate my dog's barking to know when it is hungry and get my pet dispenser to give out it's favorite food, which she will re-order from Amazon of course.

Alexa, Apple's Siri and Google Now have all been listening to us to build out voice recognition and fetching us information. As this evolves into a conversation in the intimate of settings, our perception of the experience with our devices will begin to blur.

Our experiences are nuanced and filtered by context, identity, and relevance based on location and time. This is influenced by our moods and our biases that are stored deep in our lizard brains controlling how we feel, perceive reality, get creative, solve problems, define and store as memory. Our experiences and recalling them shapes our identity of who we are and helps us grow in self-awareness. This underlying ability of living our experience as life is human intelligence. Add free will to it and it creates many billion unique combinations making it complex to replicate human experience and human intelligence. So we thought.

Internet of Things makes ordinary things all around us "smart" and collects huge volume of data that can be processed to define human intelligence. Machine Learning and Deep Learning applied to smart things changes the Human Machine Interface. We are reaching an era of questioning what is Artificial about AI after all. If human intelligence can be replicated and human experience can be deep learned, the barrier between man and machine will begin to crumble.

IoT devices are sensing our environments with gesture computing, feeling our emotions with affective computing and personalizing our experiences with recognition computing. Will this stop at Human-Machine interactions or are we helping machines develop self-awareness with personality and opinions, to become our friend, partner and part of our families. There is no escape from the trajectory of change of our perceptions of our worlds and us as humans. Or is there?

16.1 With Personal Assistants Who is in Charge?

Personal assistants come with human sounding names such as **Cloe**, Clara, **Julie**, Luka and **Amy**. The ultimate in names is **Mother.** Personal Assistants help us shop, manage our time and life routines, stay healthy and forget decision fatigue. They give us the perception of us being in charge while slowing enslaving us by learning our behaviors and preferences. Have you seen **Preemadonna's Nailbot** from TCDisrupt Battlefield? That's one robot getting ready to become the center of tween girls' slumber parties. It uses machine vision to adapt nail sizes to unleash creativity of girls as fun nail art designs. Who is in charge here? Girl or Machine?

With IoT making all things smart, our interaction with things is changing. It is a gentle reminder from our Fitbands and Apple

Health Apps to exercise more, from **imedipac** to take our pills, from **Aura** sleep monitor to sleep well and from **Nest Protect** to change our smoke alarm batteries. This becomes more pervasive when the interaction changes to assertive with **Kolibree** smart toothbrush telling parents that kids didn't brush behind their molars or **Sensoria** socks asking us to change our running style to shift balance on our heels. It enters a more private space with a **Yono Fertility band** monitoring basal temperature to help women get pregnant and gets to a crazy zone with **the True Love Bra** from Ravijour that opens only at a certain heartbeat rhythm.

16.3 Conversation as Equals

Combining gesture and recognition computing helps machines understand movement, voice and photos in context giving them the ability to perceive the world around them.

Fin and Nod help us engage naturally with our environments by mapping our hand gestures to rule based actions of turning on lights or increasing the volume of the home entertainment system. It is not far off that these devices can machine learn that we pound our fist in anger and nod to say yes. ControlAir App from Eyesight even allows me to shush my device when my phone rings. So it is not hard to imagine that we will get to more human–like interactions once our devices figure out when we roll our eyes.

Voice recognition is shifting to a two-way conversation. We can now talk to **our homes** and **connected cars** and phones not just to get driving directions but ask for advice about where to go, what to eat and what to do next. The AI being built in home hubs such as **Mycroft** allows it to understand our requests based on proximity and voice recognition. Devices are becoming part of our families, listening to us, and guiding us run our lives smoothly.

16.4 Conversation Where Humans Are Absent

Digital Genius from TCDisrupt uses Natural Language processing to let machines take on mundane tasks such as customer service and automated onboarding to services. It can also do M2M communication which is where it will get interesting where our machines negotiate with each other to find deals for us or arrange our travels or let a factory run itself from interconnected devices for our benefit. Drone couriers is another scenario becoming a reality from **CyPhy Works**. When the drone delivers Pizza, our connected home might pick it up and have a **Tellspec** track the food calories we eat.

Wearables are shifting from fitness bands to become biometric tattoos and implants that track our vitals and locations. Chaotic moon has made a temporary tattoos with sensors and conductive ink. This can be used in healthcare, military, tracking criminals and lost kids. Implants that come in the form of pills track our vitals and could talk to our doctors or medical systems leaving us out of the conversation.

Figure 25 Biometric Tattoos

Image Copyright Chaotic Moon/TechCrunch

How will our relation with the machine change as it smartens up deep learning other machine's behavior and begins to advise us?

CHAPTER 17: Bio-Identity and Blurring of reality

17.1 Augmented Reality

IoT offers the opportunity to extend the customer experience using Augmented reality.

Augmented reality blurs our senses of what is local and what is remote as we peer into a machine.

Trylive offers a remote immersive shopping experience. Qualcomm's mobile vision platform **Vuforia** lets us interact with toys before opening our gifts.

Layar creates a localized augmented experience for food, housing and entertainment and education.

17.2 Bio Payments

Biohacking company *Dangerous Things* has created a tiny NFC chip that can store 888 bytes of data and can be embedded into a human body. This has been developed into an implant chip by a team in Europe calling it Bio-payment. They use it to send Bitcoins by waving their hand over an NFC terminal. They also can use the chip as an ICE tag for first responders to read their body vitals during an emergency.

This is futuristic today but the technology for this exists and has been showcased more than once. So here is an opportunity to think about where this can be incorporated into your new product or business vision.

17.3 Affective Computing

IoT devices do not focus only on humans to understand their feelings. Researchers in North Carolina State University have created a dog harness that tells owners how their dogs are feeling based on their posture and heart beat. This is meant to help visually impaired dog owners and to help them plan when to retire guide dogs. What would be interesting is when the harness can pet the dog based on how it feels.

Figure 26 Tracker of Dog's Feelings

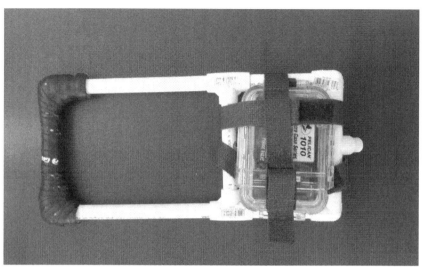

Image Copyright NC State University

Affective computing teaches machines to understand emotions with the goal to develop empathy to help them fit in socially and to take actions based on sensing our emotions. I would like Amazon Echo Alexa in my family room to behave well and eat her veggies with a smile.

But my connected car may notify other cars around it if I am driving with road rage. Wize Mirror from Semeoticons measures a person's overall health from facial recognition. If a Wize Mirror could connect to rest of my IoT devices in the retail realm it could tell my Fitbit that I am ready for binge shopping because I am walking out my stress.

Combining context with emotions, machines can take our conversations to the next level. A device on or near us all the time can notice that the girlfriend is not seen in proximity any more. Whether it will "talk" to us about it or use this information to filter its engagement with us is based on the deep learning algorithm it will develop.

CHAPTER 18: Conclusion

Let us get ready for the future with the world of Internet of Things on us and all around us.

As Entrepreneurs and Product Managers who are architecting this new world think about the privacy of the user. Think about how you will empower the user to own their content while you protect the data the customer entrusts you.

Build security at every stage of the IoT Product development process so it is not left with gaping holes in the hardware, connectivity, or software. When you connect a device to other devices in the ecosystem take responsibility for the overall security of the user.

You do not want to build a connected lock that connects to a toaster that is insecure and allows for your customer's house to be hacked.

Take care of an integrated customer experience that connects to the customer to engage them, delight them and build trust with your product.

The world of flying drones and self-driving cars is real. As the human-machine boundary is blurred, take responsibility for your product design on how you create conveniences for the customer using Artificial Intelligence. Will your product dull the senses of users by convenience to let the user give up free will for engaging experiences or will it create experiences that nurture them and not own them?

All great products solve a real customer need, one good enough for them to pay for it. So focus on how you build out your product into a business. Do you want to incrementally improve an existing experience, or do you want to grab the opportunities all around you to fundamentally disrupt and create new industries.

Today's early builders are the ones who are going to lend a shoulder to the future builders of tomorrow. So I welcome you to step towards 2020 knowing the responsibility you hold to build each product to create the fabric of our future connected world.

With the new world of IoT everywhere we can forget our keys inside the house and there is no more penalty of calling the apartment office for their extra key at midnight. However, with all the obsession with monitoring ourselves, whatever IoT will bring, if your dog chews the device up, it is a gentle reminder that you are still left in a world with a lot of uncertainty.

===============================

Epilogue by Rob Van Kranenburg

There are times when gut feeling, a clear head and deep knowledge of your area of expertise are plenty to succeed. These times are quite different. You can have all of the above and still be baffled.

We are in a time where trust, honesty and optimal efficiency and interoperability are key factors in your success, and these are built over time. There were times where you could grow old with the formula of one product, and how we long for those days!

Then again, these are times where transparency is working hard to expose unbalanced business operations. You are living in the days of the cheapest ecology of hardware (a commodity), connectivity (a commodity), software (so much fully productive open source solutions), database storage and analytics, that it would indeed be folly not to try out the ideas you have in your head.

You have grown up in the flux of data and information but you know how to find your way in it. Your skills are tuned to real-time and the network. And so you know that the only real deep skill that will truly help you is your ability to deal with insecurity. Don't worry about the future. It is not 'there', but here always.

Specialize hard but always make sure that an equally smart team that supports you surrounds you. Don't work alone and try to spread business-models over different products and services. Most important of all is that you are not afraid to learn and ask for guidance.

I guess you know this already. That is why you are here reading this book by Sudha Jamthe.

Welcome to building lasting Internet of Things Businesses with open standards that become the architects of the IoT Ecosystem.

- Rob Van Kranenburg Founder EU IoT Council

Appendix 1: Alphabetical List of IoT devices

The IoT ecosystem is buzzing with new innovations daily. As you read the list below, try to recall an IoT device you know for each alphabet, especially for the two alphabets missing any IoT Device.

Join me in being inspired by the breadth of problems solved by these devices, the global scale of their markets and how multiple products innovate to solve the same problems with a different design or feature set. If you find any IoT missing you can tell me online at http://IoTdisruptions.com. Enjoy!

A:

Apple Watch

Amazon Dash

Airfy ibeacon home automation

Artik IoT Platform from Samsung with a family of modules and open APIs

Archos a connected weighing scale

B:

BabyKick wearable device for pregnant women

BluCub Bluetooth humidity and temperature sensor

Brio Smart power outlet

Beam smart toothbrush

BITalino - DiY Hardware for Physiological Data Acquisition

BYTE Light

BACtrack – Breath analyzer to track alcohol levels

C:

Cozy Radiator Lab's century old radiators become smart

CityGram Real-time environment sensing focused on noise

Chillhub Smart wireless fridge that communicates via a mobile App

Cookoo Connected watch

CarIQ connected car IoT device for cars

Cooey - Smart blood pressure monitor

D:

The Dash Headphones with body sensor

E:

Echo from Amazon is a voice activated Internet communicator for your home

Endomondo Fitness tracking app for Blackberry Devices

Earin Wireless earbud

Emberlight Turns any light into a smart light

F:

Fitbit Plus Health Exercise Tracker

Flic Wireless smart multipurpose button

Face On the wall a face mask that responds to aural stimuli

G:

Glance Watch accessory that makes your watch smart

Glyph Personal theater

H:

Hue smart light bulb from Philips

Homey Voice controlled home automation

Hendo Smart hoverboard

Haiku Like a smart watch for your bike

Huawei Wi-Fi router ws860s

I:

Intel Smart Clip baby safety clip for car seats

IoTa GPS tracker and Motion sensor

iHealth Glucomer blood sugar monitor

iHealth Blood Pressure Wrist Monitor

iHealth wireless body analysis scale

Instant - Automatic Quantified Self tracking app

ilumi connected LED Lights

J:

Jawbone Up24

K:

Kinsa smart thermometer

Korner Home security

Kolibree Connected electric toothbrush

Kapture Audio recording wristband

L:

Livelysmart watch for seniors

Leaf from bellabeat - health tracker for holistic women health

M:

Mi band Fit band like health tracker from Xiaomi available in China, and select Asian countries.

Muse brain sensing headband

MonBaby smart baby monitor

MÜZO COBBLESTONE wireless music streaming

MapMyFitness health tracker

Moto gesture tracking ring

Mojio Humidity and Temperature control

Melon Smart headband tracks your brain activity

Moves fitness tracker

Misfit Shine Fitness + Sleep Monitor

Mota Smart ring gesture control

Mi Power strip (available in china)

Mi smart scale (available in china)

Mi TV2 (available in china) 55" LED TV

MyTraps helps farmers remotely monitor pest attacks

Misfit Bolt connected light

N:

Nakul Single use medical grade vital biometrics wearables

Nest Smart Thermostat for the connected home

Neuma Smart watch measures autonomic brain

Neveli Health Platform Analysis platform

Ninja Sphere Home control with gesture; open source platform

Nod ring that controls home by gesture

N3rd (Pronounced Nerd) is a Wi-Fi device that makes any gadget or switch smart

Nucano Smart door chime

Noke Bluetooth lock

Nike Training - Training Mobile App

O:

OORT Bluetooth bulb

Outlink Smart outlet

Orb Movement and sleep tracker

Omate Smart watch does not need phone connected for it to work

Owlet a baby shoes to monitor a baby's vitals.

OnHub smart Wi-Fi from Google

Omron Series 10 Blood Pressure and Heart Rhythm Monitor

P:

PlantLink moisture sensor for plants

PetNet Smart pet feeder

Pebble Smart watch

Pulse - Dimmable BLuetooth light with speakers

Q:

The Q smart LED bulbs with streaming music to create your own light shows.

Quirky's egg minder A smart egg tray in your fridge to manage egg stock

Quitbit Helps quit smoking

QardioArm Smart Blood Pressure Monitor

R:

Runkeeper health tracker

Ring Gesture control device

Rico Turns old phone into a robot to use for home automation

S:

Step+ Exercise tracker, part of Apple's health kit

Sleeptracker sleep pattern tracker, part of Apple's health kit

Strava GPS powered Run & ride analysis Fitness tracker

Skybell video doorbell

Satechi IQ Spectrum Smart Light

Skydrop Sprinkler controller

Samsung Gear Fit Fitness Tracker

Spray Smart meter for your shower

SITU Smart food nutrition scale

SenzIT a solution from IBM for courtrooms

Sensoria Sports Bra

Sensoria T-Shirt and Heart Rate Monitor

Sensoria Heart Rate Monitor

Sensoria Socks

Spires Measures Breath to stay stress free

Silent Partner – Quiets Snoring

T:

Think Eco a smart Air Conditioner

TrackR a tracking device to find lost items

Tile a tracking device to find lost items

TAGG Pet tracker

Tilt Blinds automation for your window

Tictrac – A Digital Health platform

U:

UBiome – personal human microbiome

V:

Vessyl Pryme connected cup tracking water hydration levels.

W:

WeMo wireless home automation system from Belkin

Withings Pulse O_x – Fitness, Sleep plus health tracker BP, Oxygen levels

Wink Home automation hub

X:

Xkuty a solar electric bike

Y:

Yono Fertility Friend, a wearable earplug to measure basal temperature for women

Z:

Zia sleep monitor

Zenobase – a service for aggregating and analyzing Quantified Self data

Bibliography

Statistic Reference

http://www.statista.com/statistics/302722/smart-watches-shipments-worldwide/

http://www.statista.com/statistics/255778/number-of-active-wechat-messenger-accounts/_)

[1.] Gartner Press Release 2013 estimated 26 Billion devices & Cisco estimates 50Bil devices by 2020https://www.cisco.com/.../IoT_IBSG_0411FINAL.pdf

[2] Gartner at Tech Europehttp://blogs.wsj.com/tech-europe/2013/05/15/opening-up-the-internet-of-things/

Wearables

Smart Watch History http://www.zdnet.com/pictures/before-the-iwatch-a-history-of-smartwatches-in-pictures/

Pebble Watch Kickstarter https://www.kickstarter.com/projects/597507018/pebble-e-paper-watch-for-iphone-and-android).

Color changing shoes - http://blog.atmel.com/2015/11/18/silent-partner-is-the-first-smart-patch-that-quiets-snoring/

Fossil Acquires Misfit http://mashable.com/2015/11/12/fossil-to-acquire-misfit/#_DZAEoIsXuq3

Sarrah Ecceleson Saving Elephants With Wearable https://plus.google.com/109879997703042555421/posts

Connected Home

Home Depot story with WINK HUB - https://medium.com/@connectedlab/lessons-learned-from-the-wink-hub-678ac3d0fb7?imm_mid=0dabb6&cmp=em-iot-na-na-newsltr_20151022#.oxmlnggni

Connected Cars

http://www.cnet.com/news/movimento-ota-mitsubishi-infotainment/

https://transportevolved.com/2014/06/16/nissan-bmw-look-adopt-teslas-charging-standard/

http://www.wired.com/2015/10/five-car-hacking-lessons-we-learned-this-summer/ (car hacks)

http://www.cnet.com/news/movimento-ota-mitsubishi-infotainment/

The Car Connectivity Consortium (CCC) http://carconnectivity.org/

http://www.cnet.com/news/movimento-ota-mitsubishi-infotainment/

Retail Industry Analysis

Beacons - https://www.mobilestrategies360.com/2015/10/29/beacon-has-eyes

Personalized Mobile Offers http://youtu.be/iXlmSjKzOeohttps://www.mobilestrategies360.com/2015/10/29/beacon-has-eyes

https://www.mobilestrategies360.com/2015/10/29/beacon-has-eyes

Eddystone https://github.com/google/eddystone

Healthcare Industry Analysis

https://wtvox.com/cyborgs-and-implantables/google-is-working-on-magnetic-nanoparticles-to-detect-cancer-cells/

https://wtvox.com/cyborgs-and-implantables/brain-computer-interface-implantable/

Smart Implants - https://wtvox.com/3d-printing-in-wearable-tech/top-10-implantable-wearables-soon-body/

http://www.cheatsheet.com/technology/what-are-wearable-devices-really-capable-of.html/?a=viewallhttp://www.cheatsheet.com/technology/what-are-wearable-devices-really-capable-of.html/?a=viewall

Understanding Standards

LoRA vs SigFox

http://www.rethinkresearch.biz/articles/on-lpwans-why-sigfox-and-lora-are-rather-different-and-the-importance-of-the-business-model/

http://www.instructables.com/id/Introducing-LoRa-/http://www.instructables.com/id/Introducing-LoRa-/

SIGFOX tutorial
http://www.radio-electronics.com/info/wireless/sigfox/basics-tutorial.php

Thread Alliance

http://www.rs-online.com/designspark/electronics/knowledge-item/eleven-internet-of-things-iot-protocols-you-need-to-know-about

http://threadgroup.org/Default.aspx?moduleId=492&PR=PR&tabI D=94&Contenttype=ArticleDet&Aid=59

http://www.networkworld.com/article/2456421/internet-of-things/a-guide-to-the-confusing-internet-of-things-standards-world.html

IoT and Edge Processing

http://events.linuxfoundation.org/sites/events/files/slides/EdgePr ocessing-allseenalliance_4x3_template_24sept2014.pdf

https://www.newscientist.com/article/dn28342-the-internet-of-caring-things/

IIoT

https://www.iotuniversity.com/2015/09/the-industrial-internet-of-things-iiot-challenges-requirements-and-benefits-by-ahmed-banafa/

http://mashable.com/2015/11/12/fossil-to-acquire-misfit/ -_DZAEoIsXuq3

Artificial Intelligence and Futuristic Technologies

http://www.theguardian.com/technology/2014/dec/09/synapse-ibm-neural-computing-chip

http://www.theguardian.com/technology/2014/dec/09/synapse-ibm-neural-computing-chip

http://amitsheth.blogspot.com/2015/03/smart-iot-iot-as-human-agent-human.html

Bio Payments

https://www.youtube.com/watch?v=2GgncP41rJ4

Case Study References

Vessyl http://www.crowdfundinsider.com/2014/07/44978-vessyl-cup-now-1-million-presales/

Nike http://uk.blastingnews.com/tech/2015/05/nike-finally-explains-why-the-fuelband-was-cancelled-00381991.html

Connect anything to anything Open Source platform
http://octoblu.com

Nest Thermostat https://en.wikipedia.org/wiki/Nest_Labs

Connected City

Smart Lighting
http://www.newscenter.philips.com/main/standard/news/press/2015/20150408-los-angeles-becomes-first-city-in-the-world-to-control-its-street-lighting-through-mobile-and-cloud-based-technologies-from-philips.wpd#.VjhdaKI7RNM

The IoT Show Archives (http://www.iotdisruptions.com)

Air Quality Measurement Atomtube CEO Vera Kozyr and James Moulding of opensensors.io
https://www.youtube.com/watch?v=WIEv6me_WGA

Future of IoT – Devices with Emotions with Prof. Ahmed Banafa
https://www.youtube.com/watch?v=NsJRRVXUjfc

Audi Brochure Hack video from The IoT Show
https://www.youtube.com/watch?v=EYMCFAjHwRM

Recommended Books

Jamthe, Sudha, *IoT Disruption Kindle book* (good beginners' intro to IoT Landscape)

Ajit Jaokar, *IoT and Data Science* (ISBN 978-1518819711)

Bernard Roth, *The Achievement Habit: Stop Wishing, Start Doing, and Take Command of Your Life* (ISBN 978-0062356109)

Gayle Laakmann McDowell and Jackie Bavaro, *Cracking the PM Interview: How to Land a Product Manager Job in Technology* (ISBN 978-0984782819)

Rich Mironov, *The Art of Product Management: Lessons from a Silicon Valley Innovator* (ISBN 978-1439216064)

Brian Solis, *X: The Experience When Business Meets Design* (ISBN 978-1118456545)

Levin, Michal, Designing Multi-Device Experiences: An Ecosystem Approach to User Experiences across Devices

Acknowledgements

First my Mom, my No.1 cheerleader who seeded magic in me to wake up each day feeling I am awesome. She continues to remind me to-date that I am special and made for some big purpose in life.

My husband Shirish brought IoT home to me, literally by hacking IoT devices all around our home for the past three years. When I wrote 'IoT Disruptions' my first IoT book, he ruthlessly challenged me to think deeper that led to this in-depth book. Thank you for expanding my horizons on IoT.

My daughter Neha Jamthe helped me find my writing style. She also brought her artistic talent by designing the book cover. This book would just be a dream without you cheering me on. I am so thankful to be your Mom and proud of your perspectives and questions that have contributed clarity to follow my heart to become an author.

My friend Hiren Patel introduced me to 'connected self' when he lent me his sleep tracker Zia for me to test out for few nights in Oct of 2013. Thank you Robert Schwentker and Hiren Patel for letting me lean on you and pushing me across the chasm of doubt when I realized the reality of publishing a print book. Thank You.

Marsha Collier the most amazing best-selling author in the whole world inspired me to write. She cheered me on after my kindle book and set the bar high for me right at the start and told me not to just write a book but publish a good quality book. Thank You for mentoring me and inspiring me.

My community of readers on LinkedIn and the loyal audience of my weekly 'The IoT Show' on YouTube! Thank You for cheering me and asking questions as I shared my research and articles.

Thanks to friends who believed in me and guided me to find answers to understand the world of publishing when I needed unconditional trust before I started writing - Natascha Thomson, Perrine Crampton and Consuelo Griego.

I am so thankful to Eric Van Der Hope, the book author's mentor who showed up in my life, handheld me and walked me through the pre-order process on Amazon. Eric knows everything anyone needs to know about successful book publishing. I am thankful for your mentorship and inspired by how much you care about every new author and give everyone time.

AWS Loft IoT Hackathon Team, Intel Evangelist Amarnath Kona, many IoT Meetups in Silicon Valley, Singapore, Amsterdam, Dom Sagella and team at iOSDevcamp, thanks for helping me build a real IoT and experience and overcome the frustrations of incompatible standards of making a real IoT Product. All my sessions onsite and online have seeded ideas for this book about how to create the best customer experience for an IoT Product. David Newman this book will be all text without your patience to educate me about image formats. Thank You.

Brian Solis, I am blessed by your friendship and your time and thoughts to write the foreword for this book.

When you set out in a new direction, you need a few people to believe in you and lots of smart people to surround you to prop you up in the new direction. When its the same set of people who are smart and believers you are doubly lucky.

I found my tribe with the IoT Council Europe under the leadership of Rob Van Den Karnenburg. Thank you Rob for leading the EU IoT council, giving me a beautiful epilogue for this book and including me among such passionate thought leaders covering every aspect of IoT. EU IoT Council members helped me start my day with a 8am call daily and brought structure to my writing life, smartened me and taught me what I needed to learn every single day.

Joachim Lindborg, Jurgen Wege, Ajit Jaokar and Ian Skerett helped me synthesize my research by challenging my thinking to develop an in-depth understanding of what is and what should be the IoT space. Bei (Jack) Zhang helped me expand my research to China.

IoT entrepreneurs Davide Vigano from Seattle, Vera Kozyr from Russia, Anaisa Rodrigues from Portugal, Aditi Chada from India, Karsten Königstein from Germany, Marc Pous from Barcelona, Thomas Serval from France, Miguel Rodrigues from Brazil, Quentin Delaoutre from France, Jonathan Carter of Netherlands, Damir Čaušević from Check Republic, Thank You for your inspiration and sharing your story and experience as you shape the IoT ecosystem with your innovations and businesses.

Hiru Létap, Susanna Maier my editors for being meticulous about grammar, punctuation, formatting and challenging me to bring out the meaning and tone of what I wanted to communicate to my readers. Thank You. You were ruthless about the many rounds of editing and I am thankful for your perseverance.

Tatyana Kanzaveli, Rich Mironov, Paul Heayn, Surj Patel, Ajit Jaokar, David Vigano, Ahmed Banafa , Scott Amyn, Thank you for your quotes.

To the many students, product managers, change agents who connected on LinkedIn and Twitter and spent hours marveling at the potential of new technologies and jobs over the years. Am thankful that you want to change the world and found me to share your dreams and brainstorm ideas.

Finally to you the reader! You have trusted me and begun this journey with me.   I am here only because of You! Thank You!

About The Author

Sudha Jamthe is a globally recognized entrepreneurial mobile product leader. Sudha loves guiding the next wave of Technology Innovation and Business Disruptions.

She is the author of two IoT books, 'IoT Disruptions' and 'The Internet of Things Business Primer'. Sudha teaches the first IoT Business course at Stanford Continuing Ed School. She hosts a weekly video show "The IoT Show". She shares a newsletter of IoT case studies that you can signup at http:// iotdisruptions.com

Sudha is a champion for Girls Who Code. She has been a venture mentor at MIT and Director of Bay Area Facebook, Twitter, Pinterest and Google+ Meetups. She also actively contributes to TechCrunch, Mashable, GigaOm and Venturebeat as a respected technology futurist. She is on the advisory board for Blockchain University and Barcelona Technology School.

Advance Praise For This Book: The Internet of Things Business Primer

"Sudha Jamthe's no-nonsense approach to IoT is refreshing, informative, and thorough. Read *The Internet of Things Business Primer* if you want to succeed in the IoT ecosystem." - **Ben Parr, Author of *Captivology* and one of Inc.'s Top 10 IoT Experts**

Sudha brings case studies from IoT Entrepreneurs and Product Builders globally and combines it with in-depth analysis from her own experience with Mobile Products to offer a must-read book about how to build a successful IoT Business. Watch out this is one of those books you are going to read and re-read many times to serve as your bible as the IoT ecosystem shapes out over the next few years."- **Myles Weissleder SF NewTech Meetup Founder**

"The Internet of Things Business Primer" is a guidebook for innovators, entrepreneurs and technology leaders looking for practical examples of best practices to build a successful IoT business. Sudha brings her own experience and the one of other entrepreneurs that have had a meaningful impact on charting the path of the IoT industry" - **Davide Vigano, CEO Sensoria**.

"Analysis of IoT from a business perspective by a seasoned business and product leader – that is what this book is all about. Sudha has done an amazing job in evaluating IoT and has shown us how to make a business out of it. This is not an easy task and Sudha has done complete justice to it." - **Pragati Rai Sr Innovation specialist Deutsche Bank & Author Android Application Security Essentials**

"Sudha is an amazing thought leader in the new and exciting field of IoT. She is talented and inspiring with her words and work. Its exciting to see her put her deep knowledge of IoT and sharp vision of the future of this trend of technology into this book" - **Ahmed Banafa, Professor San Jose State University**

" We live in a connected world that continues to evolve each day. And therein lies the opportunity to build a business. Sudha Jamthe brings her years of experience as a technologist to this comprehensive guide, applying her own experience, and drawing from others in case studies that solidify important concepts. *The Internet of Things Business Primer* is a the definitive source for anyone looking to blaze a path in the IoT world and be successful doing it." - **Frank Gruber CEO and Cofounder of Tech.co and Author Startup Mixology**

"Sudha Jamthe's new book provides the definitive roadmap for building an IoT business and navigating the forthcoming disruption across many industries with a comprehensive overview covering technology, business models and use cases"

— **Ajit Jaokar Author of Data Science for IoT and CEO Futuretext.**

"I really enjoyed Sudha's first book "IoT Disruptions" that covers the universe of opportunities that IoT is bringing to our lives. This book "The Internet of Things Business Primer" goes deeper to offer an in-depth guide and case studies for anyone who wants to learn how to build an IoT Business to accelerate the digital transformation."- **Josep Clotet, Founding Managing Director, Barcelona Technology School**

"Sudha is a great supporter of the grassroots of Silicon Valley. I had the honor to work with her, when developing Startup Weekend back in 2010 with eBay and PayPal. In this book Sudha is leveraging her unique insight to prepare the next wave of innovation and support the IoT community. This is not another book about IoT, this is a map on how to navigate the future of IoT entrepreneurship." - **Franck Nouyrigat. Co-founder Global Startup Weekend and Partner recorp**

Praise for IoT Disruptions by Sudha Jamthe

"Sudha Jamthe is a visionary, able to spot new technology trends in the social and mobile arenas. Read this book slowly and digest her advice. I suspect you will refer back to it many times." - **Marsha Collier, Best Selling Author (47 books), Computer and Technology Radio Host and Futurist**

Made in the USA
San Bernardino, CA
27 December 2015